HANDBOOK ON NATURAL DISASTER REDUCTION IN TOURIST AREAS

CONTENTS

PREFACE

To combat the attitude that people are helpless in the face of disasters, in 1989 the United Nations launched, by means of General Assembly Resolution 235, the International Decade for Natural Disaster Reduction (IDNDR).

Each decade, natural hazards kill more than one million people and leave countless others homeless. Moreover, economic losses from natural disasters are on the rise, in developed and developing countries alike. The global economic cost of disasters rose from US$ 44 000 million in 1991 to US$ 60 000 million in 1992, and constitutes a massive setback to economic growth.

With tourism now an important global phenomenon involving the movement of millions of individuals to virtually all countries on the surface of the globe, this worldwide industry is by no means immune to natural disasters.

Recognizing this, the World Meteorological Organization (WMO) and the World Tourism Organization (WTO) decided, following the signature in 1993 of a "Working Arrangement" between the two secretariats, to contribute to the IDNDR by producing a joint study of natural disaster reduction in tourist areas.

Tourism developments are often located in areas exposed to, or likely to be exposed to, sudden-onset natural disasters, in particular beach and coastal areas, river valleys and mountain regions. Moreover, should tourists become victims of a natural disaster, the negative impact on the image of the destination concerned can be both serious and long-lasting.

Aware that prevention and preparedness measures make the vital difference to casualty figures and economic losses in the wake of natural disasters, WMO and WTO decided that this Handbook should demonstrate convincingly to tourism planners, tour operators, resort managers and other involved in the tourism industry precisely how the risk of natural disasters in tourist areas can be reduced and their impacts mitigated.

In a cooperative effort never before attempted, the scientific and technological knowledge of WMO experts has been combined with the practical experience of WTO's tourism planners and managers to produce a Handbook that succeeds in guiding the reader through every stage of a counter-disaster strategy — from preparedness, through disaster onset to post-disaster reconstruction and re-launching of a tourist destination.

With the assistance (which WMO and WTO gratefully acknowledge) of the International Seismological Centre in England, and the Federal Institute for Snow and Avalanche Research, in Davos, Switzerland, the scope of this Handbook has been extended to cover all natural disasters that constitute serious hazards to tourist resorts.

These are:
(a) Tropical cyclones;
(b) Storm surges;
(c) Flooding;
(d) Avalanches; and
(e) Earthquakes.

Although the present Handbook is intended to have universal application, WMO and WTO hope it will prove of particular value to the developing countries. This reflects the concern expressed, inter alia, in AGENDA 21 adopted in June 1992 by the United Nations Conference on Environment and Development, that countries should not only warn one another of natural disasters that could affect tourists or tourist areas, but should offer assistance through appropriate technology to create low-cost disaster prevention and preparedness programmes.

In this way, nations could give practical application to another key principal of IDNDR, namely that disaster reduction measures should be a standard part of development programmes.

WMO and WTO gratefully acknowledge the inputs of all those who contributed to this Handbook and in particular to Mr Y. Boodhoo, Dr A. Hughes, Dr O. Lateltin, Mr D. W. Schnare, Mr D. O. Vickers and Prof. R. Ward for their substantial contribution to this Handbook; and also to Ms A. Boncy, Ms F. Brown, Ms B. Hurley, Ms. Deborah Luhrman, Dr L. E. Olsson, Ms. Diane Palumbo, and Mr P. Shackleford for their editorial and administrative work throughout this project.

The two organizations believe that cooperation on the present Handbook augurs well for future joint ventures in other areas which will serve to underscore the close links existing between climate, weather, travel and tourism.

G.O.P. Obasi
Secretary-General
WMO

Francesco Frangialli
Secretary-General
WTO

FOREWORD

This handbook has been prepared by the World Tourism Organization and the World Meteorological Organization.

Its main purposes are to provide technical guidance on how the risk of natural disasters can be reduced in tourist areas through adequate preparedness and how their impacts can be mitigated during and after their disasters.

This handbook is intended for, and will be of great use to, national regional and local tourism authorities, as well as to tourism planners and developers, tour operators, resort and hotel managers, and others involved in the tourism industry. In particular, it will be of great practical benefit to countries, regions and islands which are both heavily dependent on tourism and exposed to frequent natural disasters.

Madrid, April 1998

CHAPTER I

INTRODUCTION

The need to study natural disaster reduction in tourist areas may be expressed in the following terms:

(a) Tourism is now an important global phenomenon, involving the movement of millions of individuals to virtually all countries on the surface of the globe.

(b) Tourism development is frequently located in areas which are exposed to, or are likely to be exposed to, sudden-onset disasters, in particular in beach and coastal areas, river valleys and mountain regions.

(c) Because tourists do not necessarily speak the language of the country they visit, prompt communication with them of imminent, sudden-onset disasters raises a particular problem; awareness creation among tourists before their visit to a country concerning sensible precautions in the event of a sudden-onset disaster raises issues of public education.

(d) Should tourists become victims of a natural disaster, the negative impact on the image of a tourist destination could be both serious and long lasting.

(e) As developing countries participate increasingly in world tourism, the opportunity exists for design and execution of tourism plant and infrastructure in those countries to embody the latest techniques of low-cost disaster prevention and preparedness. This raises a transfer of technology issue and provides an opportunity for tourist-generating countries (mainly the prosperous, industrialized nations) to cooperate with tourist-receiving countries.

The natural disasters covered in this Handbook are caused by:

(a) Tropical cyclones (including hurricanes and typhoons);

(b) Storm surges;

(c) Flooding, including coastal, estuarine and river flooding;

(d) Avalanches; and

(e) Earthquakes.

Disaster mitigation may be achieved through risk assessment, disaster prevention and disaster preparedness. Disaster prevention may be described as measures designed to prevent natural phenomena from causing or resulting in disaster or other related emergency situations. It includes structural measures for reduction of hazard proneness of sites and non-structural measures such as public education and awareness. The general definition of preparedness is as follows: "Action designed to minimise loss of life and damage, to organize the temporary removal of people and property from the threatened location and facilitate timely and effective rescue, relief and rehabilitation."

The essential feature of the above-mentioned hazards is that they occur with a certain frequency, are characterised by sudden onset and hence could easily catch populations unprepared, but they are amenable to forecasting and prediction.

Objectives of this Handbook

The objectives of this Handbook are:

(a)　To stimulate awareness among national, regional and local tourism planners in disaster-prone areas so that they include measures for the mitigation of disasters and related aspects of preparedness in the overall planning proposals for land use and tourism project formulation;

(b)　To help tourism planners to understand the nature and extent of risks faced by tourist resorts and the local communities;

(c)　To demonstrate ways and means to reduce those risks within the limits of the socio-economic and cultural context of the resident and visiting population;

(d)　To promote and facilitate a proper assessment of risk to assist decision-making;

(e)　To provide information and checksheets on emergency planning and emergency responses to natural disasters for use by resort managers, their employees and tourists; and

(f)　To discuss the relaunching of tourism after a disaster and provide examples of tools useful to resort operators and tourism organisations to reinvigorate tourism in the wake of calamity.

Opportunities to develop and implement disaster mitigation measures occur in the wake of major disasters. This is a result of the temporary high profile of the disaster relief action and the attendant publicity focused on the international tourists involved. Advantage should be taken of such opportunities to secure resources and decisions.

The National Disaster Assistance Organization and its role

In the present Handbook it is assumed that within each receiving country a national disaster assistance organisation has been established with which the national tourism administration can establish cooperation, involving also the operational sector of tourism within the country and possibly major tour operators from the generating countries. The work of this national disaster assistance organisation will be directed towards cooperation with other organisations and receiving communities to achieve greater local self-reliance in responding to the risks from natural hazards. As the coordinating body of national counter-disaster operations, this organisation will allocate by delegation the necessary responsibilities to other agencies and departments, including the national tourism administration.

Risk assessment as part of a mitigation strategy

Risk assessment is an essential part of a disaster mitigation strategy. It will be necessary for the national government to develop a risk-assessment capability involving multidisciplinary teams operating at regional and local level. Data will be needed on hazard and disaster occurrence. This must be collected in a systematic manner with respect to the frequency, magnitude and location of hazards relevant to tourist areas. Information must also be gathered on the vulnerability of buildings and infrastructure in tourist areas. Anticipation of future hazards or disasters will be the key to effective planning. Therefore, as risk assessment is undertaken, links should be established and maintained between the physical scientists working on hazard assessment and the land use and other national planners involved in the development of tourist areas.

Concepts, inputs, data

The complex and interdisciplinary character of mitigation planning will require clear concepts. Among key inputs will be maps, data and decision-making tools, both at regional and local level. Tourism planners need to be aware of the various sources of hazard information. For example, aerial photographs and satellite images are used extensively by meteorologists, hydrologists and geoscientists, but apparently much less so by tourism planners. They are, however, a useful source of information, reducing the time and cost of scientific assessment. Bringing the physical scientist, environmentalist and tourism planner more closely together at an early stage of resort planning and disaster mitigation should therefore be encouraged and actively stimulated.

Objectives to be pursued in disaster reduction

The strategy of disaster mitigation involves complex decisions, not least because it is concerned with events which, as indicated above, occur irregularly. Investment in disaster mitigation, though generally cost-effective, may also be seen as expensive. Therefore, it is necessary to consider carefully the efficiency with which these scarce resources are used. It is essential to realize that disaster reduction is not an end in itself. It has two fundamental objectives:

(*a*)   The reduction of deaths and injuries in tourism-receiving areas;
(*b*)   The reduction of property losses (both buildings and economic assets) and environmental degradation in tourist areas.

These losses could be either direct (involving immediate damage as a result of the disaster impact) or indirect (i.e. longer-term damage to the livelihoods of populations in tourist areas through hotels and other accommodation capacity being out of service for long periods of time). Indirect losses are likely to be less tangible but, since the tourist image of the receiving country is involved, they can have a greater social and economic impact than the visible direct losses. As is well known, the media publicity that attends an accident involving even a few international tourists can have an impact on the market far exceeding the scale of the original event. Therefore, tourist areas need to pay particular attention to the indirect consequences of disasters.

UN-DHA's nine crucial concepts for disaster reduction

The United Nations Department of Humanitarian Assistance (UN-DHA) has identified nine crucial requirements and mechanisms for effective implementation of disaster reduction. These requirements apply to tourism areas as well as to other zones in countries affected by natural disasters. They are as follows:

Governmental resources
(a)   Political will and commitment;
(b)   Resources; and
(c)   Leadership, management and coordination.

Knowledge and skills
(a)   Public awareness;
(b)   Community participation;
(c)   Training and education; and
(d)   Research and development.

Restrictions and incentives
(a)   Legal and administrative framework; and
(b)   Financial incentives.
     In the course of this Handbook, reference will periodically be made to one or other of these nine crucial requirements.

From disaster to risk reduction

This Handbook is based on the notion that disaster reduction is synonymous with risk reduction. Risk, as defined by UN-DHA, means the sum of all losses that can be expected from the occurrence in a tourist area of a particular natural phenomenon. In order to introduce the consideration of risk into tourism area planning, planners require information from physical scientists and engineers which enables them to:
(a)   Assess the specific risk to various types of tourist plants within the region considered;
(b)   Compare the risk incurred in locating a given type of tourist plant at one or other of several possible sites with different hazard levels; and
(c)   Decide on appropriate planning measures to control or reduce risk.

     For the above purposes the following information will generally be needed:
(a)   Regional hazard maps at a scale of 1:50,000 or 1:100,000 showing hazard intensities expected;
(b)   Local microzoning maps showing the expected intensities for the same probability levels and time periods;
(c)   Probability distribution functions of macro intensity for each locality under study; and
(d)   Vulnerability functions, relating damage degree to hazard intensity for each structural type of tourist establishment found in the locality.
     Even this assessment of risk will only relate to the probability of losses caused directly by hazard force, however. A complete analysis of risk must also take into account: secondary losses caused by events or changes of events triggered by the hazard or by its primary damaging effects; and consequential losses resulting from death and injury, loss of function of essential services, loss of markets, interruption of tourism, etc.

Tourism in the sensitivity classification

The consequential losses resulting from damage to buildings or to elements of tourism infrastructure are determined by the sensitivity of these buildings or elements, that is to say by their contents and function, and may greatly exceed the value of the elements themselves. A tentative classification of buildings into four categories of sensitivity, according to their function, should be developed. This will include the following subdivision:
(a)   Infrastructure (roads, power grids, telecommunications);
(b)   Housing (whether modern or of traditional construction);
(c)   Economic activities (including tourism and tourism related services); and
(d)   Community services (health, administration, etc.).
     As will be seen, tourism's classification as an economic activity suggests that damage to tourism plant and facilities will have primarily economic con-

sequences for the population. Damage to community services, plant and infrastructure will have predominantly social consequences for the local population even though these can be measured in financial terms. Damage to infrastructure will affect both the temporarily resident tourist population and the permanent population of the resort. Finally, damage to housing, while it may not directly concern the tourism population, will most likely affect the population providing services for tourists.

Disaster preparedness: a good advertisement for a tourist destination

The concept of disaster preparedness is particularly important for tourist areas. An area which shows evidence of good disaster preparedness is likely to reassure international tourists considering a holiday trip to the resort concerned, while making them aware of the natural disaster risk to which the area is prone. The general definition of disaster preparedness is as follows: "Action designed to minimise loss of life and damage, to organize and facilitate timely and effective rescue, relief and rehabilitation." Measures supporting disaster preparedness include:

(a) Legislation and regulations;
(b) Readiness for disaster situations and similar emergencies;
(c) Forecasting and warning machinery;
(d) Planning and organisation for evacuation and other actions to be taken in response to warnings;
(e) Education and training of the local population, operators of tourist facilities such as hotels, tour operators and tourists; and
(f) Other organisation for and management of disaster situations, including preparation of operational plans and training of personnel involved, stockpiling of supplies and earmarking of necessary funds.

Information and education: the role of the tourism industry

The application of the concept of disaster preparedness to tourism will involve a number of measures. First, tourists and, above all, the tour operators who arrange visits to the area concerned for international tourists, should be involved in the information and education process. Second, tour operators and the tourists concerned should be involved in the dissemination of and response to warnings and any evacuation process.

This means that warnings should be communicated in a form and language which tourists can understand while tour operators should be given the opportunity to cooperate in contingency planning. Naturally, plans for evacuation also include the cancellation or postponement of inbound tourism to a region threatened by a natural disaster.

With respect to organisation for and management of disaster situations, third countries participating in relief, rescue and rehabilitation activities in the country concerned may be more strongly motivated if tourists from their own country will be among the beneficiaries of such measures.

The sociopsychology of disasters befalling tourists

The study of tourism and natural disaster reduction in tourist areas involves an understanding of the sociopsychology of tourism and natural disasters. This is a field in which very little research has been undertaken. Therefore, only a number of hypotheses can be put forward.

Market research relating both to international and to domestic tourism regularly shows that tourists, especially international travellers, have levels of educational attainment that are relatively higher than average. Tourists are therefore easier to communicate with in terms of information, awareness and educational campaigns. This is a positive aspect both for the tour operator in the country of origin — whose task is to provide general guidance and briefing to travellers on the risks in the destination concerned — and for the national tourism administration of the receiving country — whose task in communicating with tourists staying at its resorts will be correspondingly facilitated. Hotels and other places where tourists stay will have an important role and will need to establish their credentials as reliable sources of information concerning potential hazards and disasters. As will be discussed in the following chapters, information provided in hotel rooms concerning disaster situations should be clear and concise and should increase tourists' confidence that the authorities of the receiving country are experienced in managing the kind of problem experienced in the region concerned.

While the educational level of tourists is relatively high, facilitating communication and information campaigns, tourists are in an unknown environment when visiting a foreign country. While tourists may learn on repeat visits, there is a considerable danger that, through lack of experience, they may disregard warning signs of impending disaster which the local population would tend to heed. This is a matter which must be taken into account in developing educational material and warning services for tourists. It will be especially important in the case of the risk of avalanches, flash flooding and tropical storms. The provision of easy-to-understand guidance (flags on beaches or exposed coastal areas; avalanche warnings to mountaineers; meteorological warnings for campers and other tourists whose activities are likely to be affected by dangerous weather conditions or sudden floods) will assist in bridging this particular communication gap.

With the exception of those staying in condominiums or second homes, tourists are unlikely to have a financial stake in the place at which they are staying during their vacation. Therefore, if a natural disaster threatens, they do not face the prospect of losing their home. Nor are the possessions or personal effects taken on holiday by tourists likely to be especially valuable (even though the evidence of airline accidents suggests that tourists are likely to take unnecessary risks to rescue possessions and valuables). On balance, therefore, it might be predicted that, at the slightest hint of trouble or impending disaster, tourists would be willing to evacuate a resort. This would also lead to the prediction that tourists are not stayers (that group of the population identified, for example, after hurricane Camille struck the southern United States in 1969 and who preferred to stay rather than leave their homes). These considerations suggest that tourists would not be unduly reluctant to be evacuated from a disaster area, although human psychology is such that it might be advisable for tour operators to indicate that appropriate compensation would be paid for the loss of holiday time because of such forced evacuation procedures (this could be the subject of insurance). Such an argument is based on the economic principle that leisure time is a scarce resource and tourists may therefore resent interference with the progress of their holiday and even discount forecasts of adverse meteorological events. Here, the influence of the travel agency or generating country tour operator on tourist attitudes and behaviour will be important and a significant information and education role can be played by the travel trade in this respect.

Tourists at risk: dangerous forms of tourism?
A final consideration in what must necessarily be a tentative discussion of sociopsychological issues is that some tourists may, as more active forms of tourism become popular, expose themselves to risks (surfing, water-skiing, winter sports, hang-gliding, etc.) which make them particularly vulnerable should disaster threaten. The fact is that no tourist season is complete without the sad news of accidents befalling tourists engaged in some particular form of sporting or mountaineering activity and who are surprised by a sudden onset disaster or simply an adverse change in weather conditions.

Options for risk reduction relating to tourism plant and infrastructure
In this part of the introductory chapter, consideration will be given to options for risk reduction. These options will be discussed in greater detail in the chapters relating to specific disasters. However, it will be useful at this stage to indicate briefly the kinds of options which may be available and how they can be exercised.

The first option for risk reduction is the modification of the hazard through a reduction of the hazard proneness of sites. Reduction of hazard proneness may relate either to the site or to the buildings constructed on it. Site improvement aims at mitigating disaster by changing the physical characteristics of the site itself. The aim of this option is to prevent the triggering of the hazard or to regulate its impact by ground improvements or drainage or slope modification. This option is of course governed by the type of hazard involved.

The second option is strengthening of buildings, an important consideration when new hotel or accommodation developments are being planned. For the reduction of earthquake risk, strengthening is the main option. Resistance against ground shaking can also be increased and this will lead to significant risk reduction. For flood and cyclone hazards, this option can be applied to all structural types.

An associated option will be the strengthening of infrastructure at the tourist resort. The physical strength of infrastructure systems may need to be improved in order to ensure adequate functioning of day-to-day facilities and services during and after a natural disaster. This option may comprise, for example, the strengthening of bridges against lateral slide in an earthquake or against flood-induced forces.

Since areas with access to sea, river or lake shores are frequently considered attractive for tourism development, it follows that hydrological hazards are particularly significant for the industry. Therefore, options to mitigate flood risks are important for tourism developments. Civil engineers have developed efficient methods of protecting sites against floods. Technically speaking, there are virtually no flood risks that cannot be mitigated through engineering measures. But cost is a relevant factor and, in practice, engineering measures can only provide partial solutions, especially in developing countries.

The aim of protective measures is to prevent floods from reaching tourist resorts. In the case of riverine floods, this must be achieved by preventing the river spilling over the flood plain. This requires increasing the discharge capacity of the river, either by channel improvements or by the construction of dykes. Protection against heavy rainfall-induced floods is also achieved by the same means.

There are several techniques for improving the capacity of rivers. Deepening and widening the riverbed is a direct measure to increase capacity. The construction of protective dykes limits the occurrence of flooding. Likewise, an increase in pumping capacity is an option which will help reduce the impact of local heavy rainfall. Sometimes, natural drainage is problematic because of high river levels, in which case artificial emergency drainage may be installed at critical locations.

In flood-prone areas, the number of casualties is usually related to the population density of the neighbourhood at risk. A low-density tourism development is likely therefore to lead to a reduction of risk. Given that the risk in a given area depends on the specific functions in that area, tourism may be one of the functions that could be prohibited. For example, an area prone to flooding would be unsuitable for the location of a hospital because of high damage potential. In an area where the location of tourist accommodation would not be advisable it may nevertheless be possible to provide a park area or sport facilities for tourists. In any area of known flood-hazard intensity, guidelines for water-resistant building materials should be established and followed. They would be part of measures to strengthen buildings. The layout of a tourist resort will also influence risk. A resort with a complex physical layout and a lack of alternative exits could become a death-trap for tourists staying there.

In the case of cyclone-prone areas the main mitigation options for the high winds experienced during the cyclone are a reduction in the vulnerability of buildings and infrastructure and a reduction in the hazard proneness of sites. For cyclone-associated floods and storm surges, the mitigation response is similar to the response for other floods.

However, for cyclone mitigation the most important way to reduce risks is based upon the installation of an effective warning system. The appropriate response to timely warnings will lessen economic losses and much more importantly, could prevent or at least minimise human losses among the tourist population. Again, the involvement of hoteliers and tour operators will be crucial to success.

In areas affected by geological hazards such as earthquakes, the strengthening of buildings to reduce structural vulnerability is the most important measure. The following considerations are important in the case of buildings:
(a) Building configuration should be regular and symmetrical.
(b) Opening sizes should be as small as possible.
(c) The prevention of sudden collapse is more important than the prevention of damage.
(d) The rigidity of the building should be distributed uniformly.
(e) Brittle materials should be made more ductile by adding materials such as wood or steel at points of tensile stress.
(f) Reinforced concrete footings are considered to be the most effective foundations where earthquakes are concerned.

(g) Even the best earthquake design may fail if it is badly constructed. Poor quality of construction or the use of substandard materials is a significant cause of building failure.

Where infrastructure is concerned, the following factors should be taken into consideration:

(h) Many bridges are not designed to resist lateral slide; suitable techniques should be applied to new bridges as well as to the retrofitting-fitting of existing ones.

(i) Flexible pipelines for public utilities are important.

(j) If utility installations are located in the open, damage to them from falling buildings can be avoided.

In conclusion, land use regulations together with vulnerability reductions are important earthquake mitigation options. This will be discussed further in the earthquake chapter.

Planning and immediate response during the onset of a natural disaster

Despite the use of the best engineering practices, buildings and people remain susceptible to natural disasters. Thus, in addition to prevention through engineering and building construction, resort managers should have detailed plans on how to react when a disaster is imminent, or one arises without warning. There is extensive literature on emergency planning, and key references are provided at the conclusion of this Handbook on each type of disaster. Resort managers are encouraged to make full use of these references and develop detailed plans on how to deal with the various types of disasters. Annual employee training on the use of these disaster plans is equally recommended.

If, however, such detailed plans are not available when calamity strikes, the appendices of this Handbook provide checksheets that venue operators may find valuable. There are checksheets for dealing with tropical storms, floods and earthquakes. For each such disaster, there are checksheets for resort managers, employees and their families, and tourists. The employee family and tourist checksheets are prepared for immediate use and can be copied for immediate distribution.

For tropical storms and floods, the checksheets include emergency preparations that can be taken during the warning period before the calamity actually arrives. For each disaster, there is a sheet on what to do during the event itself. There is also a section for each on what to do immediately after the event to ensure safety and deal with the physical aftermath.

The basic elements of these checksheets are presented in their associated chapters within the Handbook. These discussions, however, are mere introductions to the subject. For more extensive discussions of planning and emergency response as used at sites throughout the world, reference to the literature is strongly recommended.

Relaunching tourism after a natural disaster

The severity of a natural disaster determines the intensity needed to maintain or relaunch tourism after the event. Actions to reassure the travelling public are often more significant than physical plant repair. Letting the public know the resort is open, ready for business and continuing to offer the attractions that make it a desirable tourism destination are essential elements in recovery from a disaster. It is not possible to overstate the importance of marketing the tourist destination, even after a small storm, flood or earthquake. A single negative rumour can destroy the marketability of the area, especially if there is no countering statement from the community of tourism venues at that destination. Thus, preparations for dealing with the media and with tourists scheduled to arrive after the disaster event are critical. Appendix D provides a sample press pack and includes sample question-and-answer briefing sheets useful to resort managers and tourism industry spokespeople; a draft news release, a sample fact sheet, a sample position statement and a typical free call-in hotline questionnaire.

Few tourism sites consist of a single resort. A coordinated response to a disaster from all members of the local tourism industry will be both cost-effective and will significantly increase the benefits of a relaunching effort. Whether through a chamber of commerce or a disaster response team established by the local tourism industry, it pays to find a mechanism through which to coordinate marketing and news media efforts. Detailed guidance on establishing a tourism relaunching team is provided in Sonmez (1994). Additional readings providing perspectives from throughout the world are available in the abstracts published by the Union of Local Authorities in Israel (1994). Appendix E provides a useful tool for collecting information on the infrastructure status of the tourist destination, which is extremely important to a coordinating team and those responsible for developing material for the press.

The need to know the perceptions of the tourism client is common to all disasters. A tourism destination that does not know what makes the site desirable will not know what elements must be quickly repaired and made available to the travelling public. It is these attractions that draw the public and which will serve as the basis for relaunching tourism after a disaster. Therefore, the one aspect of relaunching tourism that can and should be done well before the potential for any disaster to arise is an ongoing assessment of tourist perceptions. This is a normal element of routine tourism marketing and should be done regularly. The perceptions of potential tourists after a disaster must also be evaluated and factored into marketing associated with the relaunching effort. Also included in Appendix D is a list of precautions useful when creating the basic marketing message that will be the common thread in news media relations, advertising and responses to queries from the travelling public. The later sections of Appendix D provide guidance on basic news media relations.

CHAPTER II

TROPICAL CYCLONES AND ASSOCIATED STORM SURGES

Introduction

In recent decades people throughout the world have become increasingly alarmed by reports indicating that natural disasters are becoming more and more devastating. To a large degree this is because they are affecting ever larger concentrations of population, and increasing physical developments are more at risk. By their severity, size, frequency of occurrence and vulnerability of the extensive areas they affect, tropical cyclones and associated phenomena are among the worst natural hazards causing sudden-onset disasters. They bring strong winds and torrential rainfall and associated storm surges, floods, tornadoes and landslides. Every year several of them cause social and economic setbacks, loss of life, human suffering, destruction of property, environmental degradation and severe disruption of normal activities. Such impacts, when beyond the ability of a society to cope using its own resources, are classified as disasters. The worst of these disasters are widely reported by the media.

People are not currently able to prevent the occurrence of tropical cyclones. On the other hand, substantial progress has been made in understanding their scientific aspects and in society's ability to warn those threatened by their impacts. Measures have been identified which can substantially reduce their harmful effects. A particularly important aspect of this phenomenon, as distinct from most other natural hazards, is the worldwide availability of organized warning systems as a basis for preventive action, e.g. evacuation.

Thus lack of understanding of the dangers posed and of actions that can be taken — a fatalistic attitude and complacency — can become more potent foes than inadequacies in the ability of society to cope with the threats posed by tropical cyclones.

In an attempt to alter attitudes and change reactions to natural disasters, the United Nations General Assembly designated the 1990s as the International Decade for Natural Disaster Reduction (IDNDR) during which, for the first time, a globally concerted effort would be made to reduce the disasters caused specifically by tropical cyclones, floods, landslides and storm surges, as well as other natural hazards. Information on the IDNDR as it relates to tropical cyclones is given by the World Meteorological Organization (WMO) (1990) and complementary information is contained in Smith (1989).

In this chapter, emphasis will be placed on describing the nature of tropical cyclones and associated phenomena, their impact, the warning systems and the reduction of and response to the disasters cyclones cause, as related to tourist interests.

The nature of tropical cyclones and associated storm surges

Tropical cyclone formation, development and decay
There are always clusters of clouds over the tropical and sub-tropical oceans around the globe. When one of these clusters occurs simultaneously and at the same location with several other prerequisite conditions — which are not individually rare events — a tropical cyclone will form. The conditions for cyclone formation and development include sea-surface temperatures above 26° Celsius, high relative humidity from the surface upwards to about six kilometres, spiralling inflow of winds at low level and divergent outflow winds aloft (see Figure 1). About 80 tropical cyclones form annually, mostly during the summer or autumn months, over the ocean areas as shown in Figure 2. Thus there is a seasonal aspect to tropical cyclones. On average, the lifespan of a tropical cyclone is of the order of a week to 10 days.

Tropical cyclone structure and terminology
A tropical cyclone is the generic term for a wind storm of tropical origin with an organized rainfall pattern. When it becomes mature or intense it covers an area some hundreds of kilometres in diameter, with warm temperatures and very low atmospheric pressure at its centre, where an "eye" will form. The "eye" will be a relatively cloud-free or rain-free area of light winds with a diameter of a few tens of kilometres, surrounded by a wall of clouds, torrential rainfall and the strongest winds. As the cyclone intensifies and sustained wind speeds exceed 118 kilometres per hour (33 metres per second), it will be called a hurricane in the western hemisphere and South Pacific, a typhoon in the western North Pacific and a severe tropical cyclone or just a tropical cyclone in other regions. A picture of a tropical cyclone as photographed from outer space by a meteorological satellite is shown in Figure 3, while schematic diagrams showing the wind and other features are given in Figures 4 and 5. Tropical cyclones differ in origin, structure and other respects from extra-tropical cyclones, winter storms and monsoon storms.

Tropical cyclone motion
In broad terms it may be said that tropical cyclones move in the direction and at the speed of the environmental winds or steering current, at speeds of up to a few tens of kilometres per hour. Some frequent tracks are indicated in Figure 2. However, when the steering current is light or changing, the cyclones may move erratically, with tracks showing sudden changes in direction or even loops (see Figure 6). The speed and direction of motion of a cyclone should not be confused with its wind speed. The cyclone's direction of motion determines its track, while its speed determines the length of time before its centre reaches a location along its path (see Figure 4). Its wind speed indicates its potential for doing wind damage.

Identification
The assignment of names or other identification to cyclones greatly facilitates communication in the warning system and also in describing past events. This is elucidated by WMO (1993). Briefly, by regional agreement, people's names are used in the western and southern hemispheres while sequential numbers, denoting also the year of occurrence, and letters to indicate the area of formation, are used elsewhere. Additionally, some countries give local names to cyclones.

Impact

Not all tropical cyclones move on shore to land areas, but several of those that do cause disasters of varying severity in tourist areas. The most costly damage occurs in vulnerable areas with substantial developments and the greatest loss of life takes place at the community level in countries where mitigation arrangements are weakest. The following examples are given to show the extent — albeit in a much wider area than tourism — to which severe tropical cyclones have caused major disasters in vulnerable areas. To take two extreme cases; a single tropical cyclone killed about 300 000 people in Bangladesh in November 1970, and in 1992 hurricane Andrew caused over US$ 25 000 million damage in the United States. Other recent examples include cyclone Alibera in 1990, which wrecked virtually all the buildings in Mananjary, Madagascar, while typhoon 9025 took 500 lives and caused losses of more than US$ 350 million in the Philippines. Demolition of a building and extensive damage to a city by severe cyclones and associated phenomena are illustrated in Figures 7 and 8. For tourism the major concerns are the threat of loss of life and the destruction of tourism plant and infra-structures. Much of the environmental degradation, such as beach erosion and destruction of flora and fauna caused by tropical cyclones, is also of direct concern to tourism interests.

The length of time during which a location which is directly hit by a trop-ical cyclone (that is, the "eye" of the cyclone passes over that location) will suffer from strong winds and adverse sea conditions may vary from a few hours to more than a day. Heavy rainfall may continue for several days.

The destructive forces

The classifications of tropical cyclone intensity around the globe are all direct-ly related to wind speed. In most regions, a wind speed reaching 62 kilome-tres per hour (17 metres per second), or more is a necessary condition for a weather system to be called a tropical cyclone. There is no specific upper limit to wind speed. Much damage can be done by strong winds (see Figure 8). The wind force is related to the square of the wind speed. if the wind becomes twice as strong, its potential for doing damage becomes four times greater. The Saffir Simpson hurricane scale which is used in the United States and which describes the effects of hurricanes of different intensities is given in Table 1.

The disasters attributed to tropical cyclones are caused not only by wind but also by torrential rainfall, lightning and the associated phenomena: storm surges, floods, tornadoes and landslides. Indeed, as a cause of death, wind ranks third, behind storm surges and floods.

Storm surges. Everyone is familiar with the fact that strong winds create high waves over the open oceans and also, but to a lesser extent, over coastal waters. Some of the highest ocean waves are generated by tropical cyclones. In severe cyclones waves of 10 metres are not unusual and, less frequently, wave heights may exceed 15 metres. In addition, factors such as very strong on-shore cyclone winds, a gently sloping ocean floor profile along the coast, and extremely low barometric pressure near the centre of the cyclone, can combine to produce a storm surge, which is a rapid rise in sea-surface level near the area of strongest wind as it approaches the coastline. In areas where the astronomical tide range is large, the storm tide will be much larger if the surge occurs at the time of high tide. Such was the case with the Bangladesh cyclone of April 1992, which produced a record-breaking storm tide of about seven metres. Storm tides may also be aggravated by other factors such as occurrence in an estuarine region at the same time as a river flood, or in a bay.

The storm tide and the superimposed waves may flood beaches and coastal areas and even spread some distance inland if the topography allows. Some small islands and escape routes may be completely submerged. Historically, the greatest loss of life from tropical cyclones has occurred from storm tides in low-lying coastal areas. Figure 7 shows a picture of an apartment building before the impact of a storm tide and another of the remnants afterwards. It is reiterated that storm tides and sea action can pose the greatest threat to life for tourists in low-lying coastal areas. It is therefore of vital importance that official tropical cyclone warnings, particularly those related to storm surges and official advice on evacuation be heeded.

Other associated phenomena.
The heavy rainfalls in tropical cyclones frequently cause floods or flash floods when the cyclone moves over land. The total rainfall at a location in its path is usually greater for slow-moving cyclones, as the rainfall duration is longer. Tornadoes occur most frequently in the midwest United States in spring and early summer. However, many tornadoes have been generated in association with tropical cyclones, particularly in the southern United States and some neighbouring areas. A tornado usually appears as a funnel-shaped extension from the parent cloud to the ground, where its path may be only about half a kilometre wide and some kilometres long. However, its whirling winds at speeds of some hundreds of kilometres per hour can cause almost complete destruction along its path. The greatest risk of tornadoes associated with tropical cyclones occurs when the cyclone is making landfall. Landslides associated with tropical cyclones result from the high rainfall amounts.

Trends
Statistics on the climatology of tropical cyclones have shown an increase in the annual number forming. The Intergovernmental Panel on Climate Change has recorded the view that these increases are predominantly artificial, however, and result from better monitoring procedures; furthermore, available records do not suggest that a change to more intense cyclones are a result of climate change.

There are occasionally large variations from year to year and even from decade to decade in the numbers of tropical cyclones and in their preferred paths in specific regions. These departures from the averages have been shown in some regions to be fluctuations related to specific meteorological parameters. Periods with fewer numbers of tropical cyclones than the average may

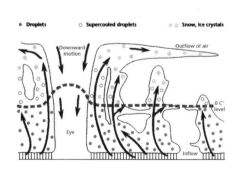

Figure 1 — Schematic cross-section of wind flow in a tropical cyclone — looking horizontally.

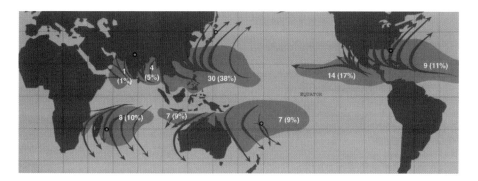

Figure 2 — Frequent tracks and annual average
numbers of tropical cyclones.

Figure 3 — Imagery from a Japanese geostationary meteorological
satellite of two typhoons in the northern hemisphere. White areas are
clouds spiralling anti-clockwise inwards to the eye (black dot).

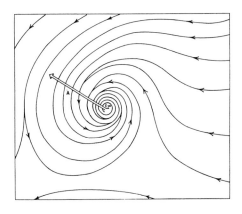

Figure 4 — The surface wind direction and the eye in a northern hemisphere tropical cyclone. The direction of the motion of the cyclone is also shown, by an arrow (A). In the southern hemisphere the wind blows in a clockwise direction.

be expected to be followed by periods with increased numbers of cyclones and seasonal forecasts are being issued on a regional basis in the western hemisphere. However, trends in the frequency of occurrence, tracks and intensity of tropical cyclones have not been definitively identified.

Detection, monitoring, forecasting and warning
Effective early warnings are major factors in tropical cyclone disaster preparedness. Establishment of warning services worldwide is a realistic goal. Indeed, there is now a warning service covering all areas directly affected by tropical cyclones. The responsibility for provision of the warning service for each country and its coastal waters rests in principle with the national Meteorological Service of that country. In a relatively small number of instances where the national service is not able to meet these responsibilities, then by agreement warnings are provided by another Meteorological Service in the region. Primary responsibility for warnings for those on the high seas and for civil aviation is selected by Meteorological Services, each for a specified area until complete coverage has been achieved.

Because of the complexity of atmospheric processes, lack of complete scientific knowledge of the structure, dynamics and behaviour of cyclones or inadequacies in the data available in real time, there are obviously limitations in the forecasting of cyclones. These shortcomings lead to a level of uncertainty in the forecast and the need for a degree of over-warning, which usually increases when a longer warning lead time is to be provided.

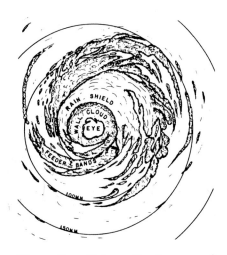

Figure 5 — Schematic diagram of the cloud structure of a northern hemisphere tropical cyclone — looking down from above and as it would appear on a radar picture.

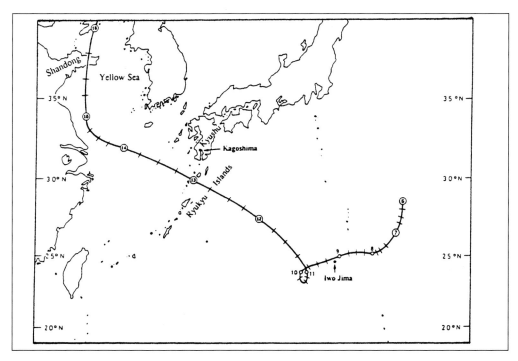

Figure 6 — Tracks of two tropical cyclones showing erratic motion (numbers are dates, starting from formation on 16 and 18 August 1986).

Nevertheless, there will always be users who could benefit from more lead time than is currently given. Thus there will be a continuing value in further improving even the state-of-the-art forecasting and warning systems. The requirement for increased facilities and application of modern technology is strongest in those countries where most deaths from cyclones occur.

The progress already made must be kept in mind. To take an extreme case, it has been reported that early this century hurricane warnings were displayed along the US coast from Charleston, South Carolina to Brownsville, Texas for a hurricane that eventually made landfall in Bermuda. Today the average error in the 24-hour forecast position is of the order of 200 kilometres. With the advent of meteorological satellites and their present complete coverage of tropical ocean areas, cyclones no longer go undetected and all are regularly monitored. The statistics indicate a death toll decreasing with time, despite population increases in vulnerable areas (see Figure 9). This can be attributed in large part to the improvements in warnings and response to warnings. At the same time, both the damage statistics, and certainly the amount and value of property at risk, have been rising, in some places at alarming rates (see Sheets, 1994). It is a complex and difficult task to estimate the reduction in damage attributable to response to warnings. However, the damage caused by tropical cyclones is now certainly much less than it would be without the combined warnings, response to warnings and preventive measures.

**Figure 7(a) — Demolition of a building by a storm tide:
Twenty-five people decided to ignore the warnings and have
a "hurricane party" in this apartment building...**

Various activities of national Meteorological Services are coordinated by WMO. Forecasts and warnings are prepared within the framework of WMO's World Weather Watch programme (WWW). Under this programme, meteorological observational data provided nationally, data from satellites, and products provided by designated centres are exchanged around the globe. In the past decade or two, regional cooperation and coordination have contributed to the upgrading of tropical cyclone warning services, with specialised products being provided by centres designated under the WWW and the associated Tropical Cyclone Programme. The flow of data and products is illustrated in Figure 10. Progress is also being made in other activities, such as training of personnel, transfer of technology and installation of modern facilities.

Reduction of tropical cyclone disasters
Overview
The main components of a comprehensive and integrated approach to reducing tropical cyclone disasters are generally considered to be:
(a) Risk assessment, including hazard and vulnerability evaluations;
(b) Disaster prevention, both structural and non-structural measures; and
(c) Disaster preparedness, including emergency planning and response to warnings, with actions taken in an interrelated and coordinated manner.

**Figure 7(b) — ...the next day, following a hurricane and
storm tide, 23 of them were dead.**

Tropical cyclone disaster reduction in tourist areas relates not only to tourists but also to the country's and local area's social and economic development and its sustainability, as well as to its environment. Many of the basic disaster reduction activities are taken at national and local levels.

The tourism industry should cooperate and participate in such activities. Particular attention should be given to disaster prevention (e.g. in tourist accommodation construction and awareness programmes for tourists) and in preparedness planning (such as training of personnel, dissemination of warnings, response to warnings and testing of plans).

In many developing countries funds are limited and decisions are based on the relative priorities of the many requirements. In practical terms disaster reduction often does not obtain a sufficiently high priority; hence it does not command the needed resources. This is because the benefits, although substantial, will only be derived in the future, at some uncertain date. Disaster reduction is compared, to its disadvantage, with other needs which promise immediate and often quantifiable benefits. In such cases the tourism industry should use its influence to promote greater recognition of the importance of disaster reduction, and of the need to accord it a higher priority, for the good of local communities and the industry. Special emphasis should be placed on meeting the requirements for provision of risk evaluation, upgrading the tropical cyclone warning services and obtaining the full benefits of response to warnings.

Figure 8 — Damage to dwellings and domestic plantation by a severe tropical cyclone. (Photo: J. S. Tyndale-Biscoe)

The main concerns for tourism are protecting tourists, avoiding loss of life, and safeguarding tourism plant and infrastructures. Generally, protection of infrastructures is a national responsibility but it should still be of concern to the industry.

Hazard, vulnerability and risk evaluation
Risk evaluation should be the first step in cyclone disaster reduction. The occurrence of a tropical cyclone represents a hazard but does not by itself cause a disaster for tourism. Tourism development is a necessary prerequisite. The impact of the cyclone and its consequences depends on the vulnerability of the location. The combination of assessments of both the cyclone hazard and locational vulnerability leads to risk evaluation, which is ideally displayed on risk maps (details are given in Plate [1994] and UNDRO [1991]).

Risk evaluation should take all risks into account and should, for example, involve combined analyses of storm surge and river flood. Risk evaluations often serve as the bases for assessing the consequences in monetary terms or in terms of potential loss of life, consideration of the options that are available, and hence decisions on disaster reduction actions.

Risk evaluation can play an important role not only as a basis for decisions on disaster prevention and preparedness actions by tourism interests, but also for economic and physical planning and in the equitable design of insurance schemes.

Provision of risk evaluation should, it is contended, be the responsibility of the local authorities and involve interdisciplinary input, including information from tourism planners on present and planned tourism plant and tourist populations. Risk evaluations should be updated as more data become available. Where they are not yet available, the tourism industry should press for the evaluations to be made. In the meantime, decisions on disaster reduction should still be made — actions based on qualitative assessments are better

TABLE 1
The Saffir Simpson hurricane intensity scale*

One   Winds 74-95 m.p.h. (64-83 kts, 119-153 km h^{-1}, 33-42 ms^{-1})
      No real damage to building structures; damage primarily to unanchored
      mobile homes, shrubbery and trees.

Two   Winds 96-110 m.p.h. (84-96 kts, 154-177 km h^{-1}, 43-49 ms^{-1})
      Some roofing, door and window damage to buildings; considerable damage
      to vegetation, exposed mobile homes and piers. Small craft in unprotected
      anchorages break moorings.

Three Winds 111-130 m.p.h.(97-113 kts, 178-209 km h^{-1}, 50-58 ms^{-1})
      Some structural damage to small residences and utility buildings with a minor
      amount of curtainwall failures; mobile homes are destroyed.

Four Winds 131-155 m.p.h.(114-135 kts, 210-249 km h^{-1}, 59-69 ms^{-1})
      More extensive curtainwall failures with some complete roof structure failure
      on small residences.

Five Winds greater than 155 m.p.h. (135 kts, 249 km h^{-1}, 69 ms^{-1})
      Complete roof failure on many residences and industrial buildings; some
      complete building failures with small utility buildings blown over or away.

* based on the hurricane's present intensity

than no action at all. Actions may be taken on the basis of hazard assessments derived from long-term meteorological records obtained from the
national and other Meteorological Services and available vulnerability data, or
at least by taking stock of past experiences of the impacts and consequences
of cyclones.

Disaster prevention
The term tropical cyclone disaster prevention is used in practice to describe
activities designed to provide protection from the impact of cyclones. These
include structural measures — engineering and other physical protective
measures for reducing vulnerability of sites — and non-structural measures
such as legislation and codes on land use, urban planning and building. It
refers to actions that may be taken well in advance of the occurrence of the
cyclone and usually also includes public awareness and disaster insurance
(see ESCAP/WMO/LRCS, (1977).
     Structural measures. The construction or establishment of tourism
plants, including tourist accommodation, should be based on risk assessments and touristic appeal. These may be conflicting factors, a commonly
encountered example being the attraction of tourists to beaches, some of
which may be areas where occurrence of storm tides is likely. The hazard
assessment should estimate the probability of occurrence of tropical cyclones
and their recurrence intervals, that is the average time interval between occur-

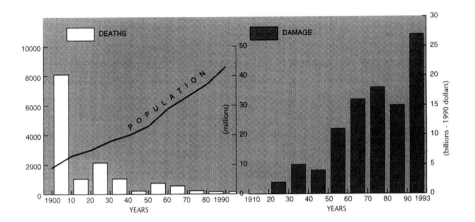

Figure 9 (a) — Decreasing death toll due to hurricanes in the United States...

Figure 9 (b) — ...despite increasing population in hurricane-prone areas such as Florida's coastal counties.

rences, of the parameters (winds, storm tides, etc.) of specified strengths. The risk evaluation takes into account the consequences if the event should occur. These should be factors in taking decisions on location of installations and the design of constructions, including buildings and physical protective barriers. The latter may vary widely, from sea walls and windbreaks to building shutters. Thus, in broad terms, design criteria should be based on the recurrence intervals expected, and should be largely influenced by a reasoned judgment balancing the risk of loss of life and property and the investment required. Risk evaluation is also useful for making decisions on effecting disaster insurance.

As long as the arguments in favour of tourist activity in a vulnerable area are stronger than the arguments against it, tourism development is likely to take place. Disaster reduction must therefore seek to apply technical solutions through structural measures, within the limits of economic viability. Generally, as the protection from risk is increased so is the cost, but safety of people must also be considered. Implicitly, a degree of risk has to be accepted. This may be larger than desirable if the costs are very high. Alternatively, or more usually as additional actions, disaster preparedness must be increased, with the main emphasis on saving lives rather than property.

Non-structural measures. National authorities should have the responsibility for enacting legislation or making regulations on land use, urban planning and construction as well as promulgating building codes. Full compliance by the tourism industry is strongly advocated. It is in the long-term interest of the industry itself as well as of the community. In the absence of such legislation and codes, rational decisions on tourism planning should prevail and developments in risk areas should be preceded by careful study and planning, and accompanied by appropriate prevention and preparedness measures. The authorities and the tourism industry itself must be concerned about individual developers who seek to make a quick profit without regard to long-

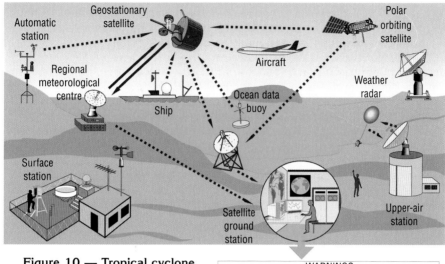

Figure 10 — Tropical cyclone warning system.

WARNINGS
from National Meteorological Centres to disasters preparedness organizations, information media, tourists interests, and other users of warnings

term security of investments, or even more importantly, the safety of tourists. Actions to be taken to prevent or at least strongly discourage such practices will depend on local policies, practices and the circumstances.

In any event, tour operators should establish active awareness and information programmes for tourists. It is essential that individual tourists have at least some information on tropical cyclones and associated phenomena, a basic understanding of the dangers they pose, the prevention and preparedness measures implemented and the action that they may need to take.

It is probable that dissemination of information on disaster reduction measures in force will diminish tourists' concern for their safety and be a good advertisement for a destination. It may be noted that information, including posters and other material to support these programmes, is normally available from the national authorities (see Figure 11) or from regional and international disaster management organisations. However, tour operators, who usually understand the tourists better, may wish to design their own material based on this information which is suited to the requirements as they perceive them.

Disaster preparedness

Tropical cyclone disaster preparedness comprises actions designed to minimise loss of life and damage, and includes warnings and response to warnings. These actions may also facilitate post-disaster activities (see ESCAP/WMO/LRCS [1977]).

Disaster preparedness should be based on risk evaluation and should take into account the assessment of the cyclone hazard and the vulnerability of the specific area after allowing for the impact of prevention measures. Its main aim is the security of tourists, also with attention to reduction of property damage.

Planning. Although most of the preparedness measures would be put in force only in the hours immediately preceding the onset of a tropical cyclone, preparedness planning, training, making contingency arrangements and testing of the measures should take place much earlier. Plans should be made for the tourism industry to promote and participate in the dissemination of warnings on a timely and reliable basis to ensure that the tour operators, their staff and individual tourists are informed. Response to warnings should be carefully planned, with particular attention to items such as:

(a)   Ensuring tourists are in a safe place by the onset of and throughout the tropical cyclone's passage;

(b)   Evacuation where appropriate — who, how, when and to where;

(c)   Stockpiling of supplies food, water, etc;

(d)   Search and rescue and medical attention;

(e)   Preparing for the cyclone, erecting of shutters, securing outdoor small objects, etc;

(f)   Preparation of emergency communication system;

(g)   Coordination with transport and traveller venue operators;

(h)   Development of employee and guest rosters, in the latter case paying special attention to their home addresses and next destinations; and

(i)   Post-storm inspections and safety measures.

It is important that warnings reach those in small craft at sea, those in trailer or mobile homes and others who are particularly at risk. Actions to be taken vary from place to place and depend on the circumstances. To assist resort managers, a checklist of emergency preparations is provided in Appendix A. These cover: protecting the physical plant; emergency shelter coordination; communications; employee coordination; guest roster maintenance; evacuation coordination; travel assistance and transport coordination; and security coordination. Other sections of the appendix provide venue managers with checksheets useful during and immediately after a tropical storm. Appendix B provides checklists for tourists that can be copied directly and distributed by venue managers. Pages B-1 and B-2 cover what to do before, during and immediately after tropical storms. Similar checksheets for employees and their families are presented in Appendix C.

Tourism managers should make the necessary plans to ensure that their staff are fully trained and motivated to carry out their respective roles in preparedness actions, particularly in dissemination of warnings, emergency arrangements and other responses to warnings. Training material should be available from the local authorities.

In regard to evacuation, the likely state of communications, roads, bridges, airports, etc. and changes or breakdowns, caused for example by the onset of floods, lightning and congestion, should be considered and contingency plans should be drawn up.

Plans should be made in coordination with local authorities and should be periodically reviewed or tested. The suitability of the new location upon evacuation should be checked in the planning stage. Arrangements should be made for records to be kept and advice to be given out when possible.

Implementation of preparedness measures. Implementation should follow a pre-prepared plan to avoid a last-minute hurry or leaving tourists unready. Some activities may require more time than the lead time given in the warnings. In such cases they should commence before warnings are issued, to ensure completion in good time. Warning bulletins usually contain information which allows estimation of the time of onset of the cyclone, if it hits the locality. Otherwise, advice may be sought from the national Meteorological Service.

When cyclones are imminent, tourists have some advantages over residents, such as a place of origin to which they could return if appropriate. In addition, they are more responsive to evacuation arrangements. On the other hand, they have some disadvantages, such as probably little or no experience of a cyclone and limited familiarity with the place, the local practices and maybe even the language. These problems require special attention. Also, morale is an important factor.

Relief, rehabilitation and reconstruction

For the tourism industry, the main post-disaster concerns are with rehabilitation, that is restoration of normal activities and repair or reconstruction of damaged tourism plant and infrastructures. It is possible that some tourists will emerge from a cyclone disaster disappointed by a ruined holiday and the discomfort experienced. Keeping up morale during the cyclone can help tourists to recognise that the efforts made on their behalf are prompted by regard for their safety and their value to the industry, and to foster feelings of concern for the host community. Rehabilitation should aim at a return to services as usual as soon as possible, but this may depend on the severity of the disaster and the time taken to restore infrastructures. In reconstruction the aim might be to make the facilities more cyclone-resistant rather than merely restoring them.

As was discussed in the introduction to this Handbook, repairing the physical plant is only one element of the recovery from a tropical storm. Relaunching tourism will be critically dependent on how well the tourism site is portrayed by the media, and how well the tourism industry develops and spreads a message to market its site. Appendix D provides detailed guidance on marketing and news media relations. Appendix E can be used to assess the status of the infrastructure essential to tourism.

While infrastructure repair and marketing are dependent on available funding, funding assistance varies widely from nation to nation. Tourism resorts should seek assistance from their respective regional, state and national government officials, who will have information on funding availability and procedures.

PAGASA FORECASTS AND WARNINGS

Public Storm Signal No. 1

Public Storm Signal No. 2

Public Storm Signal No. 3

Public Storm Signal No. 4

PIIAS/PAGASA/DOST   AUGUST 1992

Figure 11 — Example of cyclone poster used in India.

HURRICANE SAFETY RULES

Hurricane advisories will help you save your life . . . but you must help.
Follow these safety rules during hurricane emergencies:

1. **Enter each hurricane season prepared.** Every June through November, recheck your supply of boards, tools, batteries, nonperishable foods, and the other equipment you will need when a hurricane strikes your town.

2. **When you hear the first tropical cyclone advisory,** listen for future messages; this will prepare you for a hurricane emergency well in advance of the issuance of watches and warnings.

3. **When your area is covered by a hurricane watch,** continue normal activities, but stay tuned to radio or television for all National Weather Service advisories. Remember, a hurricane watch means possible danger within 24 hours; if the danger materializes, a hurricane warning will be issued. Meanwhile, keep alert. Ignore rumors.

4. **When your area receives a hurricane warning:**
   Plan your time before the storm arrives and avoid the last-minute hurry which might leave you marooned, or unprepared.
   Keep calm until the emergency has ended.
   Leave low-lying areas that may be swept by high tides or storm waves.
   Leave mobile homes for more substantial shelter. They are particularly vulnerable to overturning during strong winds. Damage can be minimized by securing mobile homes with heavy cables anchored in concrete footing.
   Moor your boat securely before the storm arrives, or evacuate it to a designated safe area. When your boat is moored, leave it, and don't return once the wind and waves are up.
   Board up windows or protect them with storm shutters or tape. Danger to small windows is mainly from wind-driven debris. Larger windows may be broken by wind pressure.
   Secure outdoor objects that might be blown away or uprooted. Garbage cans, garden tools, toys, signs, porch furniture, and a number of other harmless items become missiles of destruction in hurricane winds. Anchor them or store them inside before the storm strikes.
   Store drinking water in clean bathtubs, jugs, bottles, and cooking utensils; your town's water supply may be contaminated by flooding or damaged by hurricane floods.
   Check your battery-powered equipment. Your radio may be your only link with the world outside the hurricane, and emergency cooking facilities, lights, and flashlights will be essential if utilities are interrupted.
   Keep your car fueled. Service stations may be inoperable for several days after the storm strikes, due to flooding or interrupted electrical power.
   Stay at home, if it is sturdy and on high ground; if it is not, move to a designated shelter, and stay there until the storm is over.
   Remain indoors during the hurricane. Travel is extremely dangerous when winds and tides are whipping through your area.
   Monitor the storm's position through National Weather Service advisories.

Beware the Eye of the Hurricane

If the calm storm center passes directly overhead, there will be a lull in the wind lasting from a few minutes to half an hour or more. Stay in a safe place unless emergency repairs are absolutely necessary. But remember, at the other side of the eye, the winds rise very rapidly to hurricane force, and come from the opposite direction.

---

5. **When the hurricane has passed:**
   Seek necessary medical care at **Red Cross** disaster stations or hospitals.
   Stay out of disaster areas. Unless you are qualified to help, your presence might hamper first-aid and rescue work.
   Drive carefully along debris-filled streets. Roads may be undermined and may collapse under the weight of a car. Slides along cuts are also a hazard.
   Avoid loose or dangling wires, and report them immediately to your power company or the nearest law enforcement officer.
   Report broken sewer or water mains to the water department.
   Prevent fires. Lowered water pressure may make fire fighting difficult.
   Check refrigerated food for spoilage if power has been off during the storm.
   Remember that hurricanes moving inland can cause severe flooding. Stay away from river banks and streams.

Tornadoes spawned by hurricanes are among the storms' worst killers. When a hurricane approaches, listen for tornado watches and warnings. A tornado watch means tornadoes are expected to develop. A tornado warning means a tornado has actually been sighted. When your area receives a tornado warning, seek inside shelter immediately, preferably below ground level. If a tornado catches you outside, move away from its path at a right angle. If there is no time to escape, lie flat in the nearest depression, such as a ditch or ravine.

HURRICANE WATCHES MEAN A HURRICANE MAY THREATEN AN AREA WITHIN 24 HOURS.

HURRICANE WARNINGS MEAN A HURRICANE IS EXPECTED TO STRIKE AN AREA WITHIN 24 HOURS

NOAA/PA 70023 1974   For sale by the Superintendent of Documents, U.S. Government Printing Office. Washington. D.C. 20402. Price 25 cents

☆ GPO · 1974 O · 551-474

Figure 12 — Hurricane safety rules — United States example.

CHAPTER III

FLOODING: COASTAL FLOODING, ESTUARINE AND RIVER FLOODING

Introduction

The early years of the United Nations International Decade for Natural Disaster Reduction (IDNDR) have been marked by a succession of dramatic press and TV images of flood disasters, many of them in tourist areas. There has indeed been an unusually massive destruction of tourist and commercial recreation facilities in both inland and coastal areas of Western Europe in recent years. For example, in September 1992 cars and caravan trailers were swept like toys along swollen rivers in France and Italy. Major flooding of tourist areas in 1992 also occurred in Florida, although here the disaster was less surprising because of the perception that Florida is, in this respect, more "disaster-prone" than Western Europe.

Other recent flood disasters occurred in January 1990 with extensive flooding in Cairo, Egypt after the heaviest rainfall in many years. In April flooding in the Darling basin in Australia extended from central Queensland to southern New South Wales. In September 100 000 inhabitants of Seoul were left homeless after one of the worst downpours in the history of the Republic of Korea. Worse was to come in 1991 as Bangladesh again experienced major loss of life and catastrophic levels of homelessness during flooding in both May and September. Similar disasters occurred in China and India in July and in the Philippines in November. In September 1992 the Punjab of Pakistan and parts of northern India were flooded after torrential rain.

The fact that not all these examples occurred in typical "tourist areas" must be considered in the light of two important and relevant observations. First, floods occur in the same way in tourist areas as in other areas; accordingly, the comments which follow in this section are predicated on the basis that tourism managers need to understand the basic nature and mechanisms of floods and the impacts of flood disasters in order to manage tourist areas safely and effectively. Second, the tourist industry is growing and extending so rapidly, e.g. to many countries in Africa, to the Indian subcontinent, China, the Pacific tropics and even Antarctica, that it would be unwise to exclude any country as a possible tourist location by the early years of the 21st century.

The nature and causes of floods

Floods are probably the most widespread of the natural disasters discussed in this Handbook and constitute part of a familiar litany of disaster-prone areas. Although some countries have been singled out in this book, there are in fact no parts of the world in which flooding does not occur as rivers overflow their banks, low lying coastal areas are submerged beneath saline or brackish water, or mountain settlements are engulfed by great outpourings of melting snow and water. Indeed, the flooding of low-lying land is inevitable in the sense that the size and capacity of river channels is adjusted to average flows and not to flood flows. When the latter occur the capacity of the channels is overtaxed and the extra water spills naturally onto the adjacent flood-plain areas. Similarly, in low-lying estuarine and coastal areas, inundation is inevitable if the normal tidal range is exceeded.

In other words, the causes of floods are not difficult to understand (see Figure 1). Apart from the rare effect of landslides or dam failures, river floods are caused almost entirely by climatological factors, i.e. either excessively heavy and/or excessively prolonged rainfall or, in areas of snow or ice accumulation, by periods of prolonged and/or intense melt. Estuarine and coastal flooding is also invariably attributable in part to climatological factors, e.g. the coincidence of a large fresh-water discharge and very high tides in an estuary, or of high tides and storm surge conditions along low-lying coastal areas.

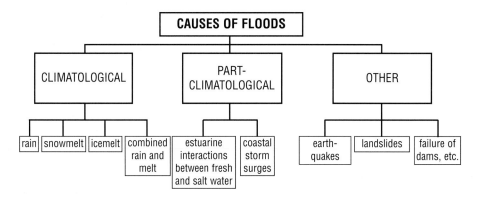

Figure 1 — Causes of floods

The severity of flooding may be measured or characterised in a variety of ways. The most commonly used indices are the depth and the duration of inundation, and the velocity of the floodwaters. Inundation becomes particularly hazardous, for example, when the depth of floodwater exceeds one metre and its velocity exceeds one metre per second. In most cases, the longer the duration of inundation the greater is the potential for damage in both urban and rural areas. The seasonality of flooding is also important. In rural areas, for example, floods in the dormant season may do more good than harm — the Nile flood was, after all, eagerly anticipated by flood-plain agriculturists for millennia; in tourist areas the most dangerous combination is obviously when the main flood season coincides with the main tourist season. Fortunately, in many tourist locations this is not the case, e.g. the "top end" of Australia's Northern Territory, where the tourist influx to Kakadu National Park and other scenic attractions is concentrated in the dry season; or in the urban tourist complexes of the U.S. eastern seaboard, where storm-surge flooding tends to occur after the holiday-makers have returned home.

The severity of flooding may be intensified by many factors, singly or in combination. River floods are normally greater for a given amount of rain when the river catchment area is in its least receptive condition. This may simply mean that the catchment is already just about as wet as it can be when the rainfall begins; or that the ground surface has been modified and compacted through, for example, overgrazing or urbanization or forest clearance.

In each case the falling rain is unable to soak in and will instead quickly run off into the stream and river channels. River flooding is also more severe when seasonally high discharges of meltwater during the late spring and early summer are accentuated by torrential rain falling on the melting ice cover or snowpack. Estuarine flooding is much more severe when a major storm surge coincides with peak freshwater discharge into the estuary from the contributing river catchments. Their severity will be intensified when the peak of the surge coincides with a spring tide maximum. Tropical storms (cyclones, typhoons, hurricanes) cause some of the most disastrous flooding associated with storm surges (see Chapter II). Some surges occur on non-funnelling coastlines, usually because of a combination of high tides and large waves generated by strong winds in the open ocean, e.g. Caribbean hurricanes approaching the southern and eastern coasts of the United States.

There is much debate about whether the severity and/or frequency of flooding is getting worse. On the whole the evidence for more severe precipitation or melt conditions, even over comparatively localised areas, is confused and confusing. Major climate changes have taken place in recent geological time, and will continue to do so during the next few millennia. In part, such changes are likely to be modified by anthropogenic factors, e.g. global warming, which may have a comparatively dramatic short-term effect, through the impact of sea-level rise, on the severity and frequency of flooding in many coastal and island areas. In the (IPOC) scientific assessment of climate change (Houghton, Jenkins and Ephraums, 1990) it is estimated that, with "business as usual," global mean sea level will be 8-29 cm higher by the year 2030 and 21-71 cm higher by the year 2070. This may not sound a great deal but it will severely exacerbate the problems of coastal flooding in island countries such as the Maldives, in deltaic countries such as Bangladesh, and in other important tourist destinations such as Venice and Florida. In those areas where the coastline is slowly sinking, for tectonic or eustatic reasons, the problems will be even more severe.

Flood disaster impacts and trends

Inundation by water is a common occurrence in the sense that, in a given area, it may occur frequently (i.e. at least once a year) and it may sometimes result from relatively modest occurrences of rainfall, melting ice and snow, or weather disturbances in the case of storm surges in coastal areas.

That floods cause so much loss of life and property may therefore be surprising but this is partly because they are often sudden-onset events, e.g. flash floods resulting from torrential downpours, and partly because the immediate causes are themselves difficult to detect, e.g. the internal melt processes within a glacier or snow cover which lead to the sudden collapse of the ice mass and cause yokelhaups or slush flows. Even when floods are relatively slow-onset events, e.g. those events in the lowland areas of major river basins which are caused by seasonal snow melt in the headwaters several weeks or even months earlier, the lowland population may be caught unprepared if adequate warnings have not been disseminated or if the resources to respond appropriately to these warnings are not available.

Increased flood detection may be explained by continuing improvements in monitoring systems and international communications (Smith, 1992). More surprising is the increasing damage from flooding in both developed and developing countries, with deaths also increasing in the latter. This runs counter to the evidence that flood frequency is not increasing and to the enormous investment in flood disaster reduction, and may be influenced by several factors. Increasing population growth and large-scale movements of population for political or economic reasons, especially in the less developed countries (LDCs), may result in a new residential development on marginal, high-risk land such as flood plains. Economic growth often results in extensive new tourist, industrial and commercial development on easily developed flat land, including flood-plains and other flood-prone areas. Increasing pressure on land resources, leading to environmental degradation through deforestation and over-cultivation, may exacerbate the flood risk. In addition, new technology and new investment in disaster reduction may in itself increase the potential for damage and death if that technology fails (Smith, 1992). This problem appears to be especially acute, and has often been referred to as the "levee effect." In other words, investment in a wide variety of flood disaster-mitigation techniques creates a largely false sense of security in the "protected" communities which encourages further development — including tourism development — of flood-prone areas. When, inevitably, a higher magnitude flood eventually exceeds the capacity of the mitigation technique, the resulting losses are much greater than they might have been had that sense of security not been engendered.

In tourist areas the flood disaster risk is exacerbated by the unfamiliarity of tourists with the local language, and by their geographical isolation from the principle administrative machinery, especially in the case of "mobile" tourists such as caravanners, campers, walkers, etc. In addition, not only may the seasonality of both flooding and tourism coincide, but it is frequently the case that the very characteristics of the landscape which tourists find most attractive are those which contribute significantly to the flood risk.

Seasonal character of flooding and of tourism

Although in most parts of the world river floods can occur at any time of year, they tend to be most numerous in the wet season. In the case of rainfall-produced floods, the wet season is either the rainy season or, in areas of uniform precipitation, the season of maximum catchment area wetness, associated with low temperatures and minimum evaporation. As has already been observed, tourists tend to avoid the wet season in hot climates, as being uncomfortable and "sticky," and the winter season in cool climates, as being too cold. In high altitude and high latitude areas, maximum flood frequency will normally be associated with the melt season. Certainly, large rivers, which normally show marked seasonal characteristics, invariably attain their peak flows during these seasons. On smaller streams, however, the most severe flooding may be associated with intense convectional storms, which can occur at any time.

In mountain areas flooding caused by such storms can be particularly severe if there has previously been an unusually late fall of snow, e.g. the Swiss alpine floods of July and August 1987 (Askew, 1992). Particular dangers are faced by tourists in such locations, since summer visitors to alpine environments tend to be attracted by the dramatic scenery and may be less knowledgeable about the physical environment and its hazards than are winter sports visitors.

Other areas, for example many desert areas, may show no marked sea-sonality of river flooding, i.e. there is an apparently random distribution of flood risks which, especially when flood events are rare, poses major problems for flood prediction and forecasting. In the case of coastal and estuarine floods, the period of maximum flood risk is associated with storm surges generated during the major storm season.

Tourist plant development in areas vulnerable to flooding

The effectiveness and appropriateness of response to flood hazard varies widely both between and within developed and developing countries. Not surprisingly, nations subjected frequently to major flood disasters may lack the social and economic stability to handle those disasters. In part, the nature of the flood hazard determines the social and economic response, rather than vice versa. When almost half of a delta nation such as Bangladesh is inundated, as in the floods of 1987 and 1988, where else can its 110 million inhabitants go? And what realistic chance is there of making more than a minuscule impact on future flood risk, no matter what the level of financial investment in flood mitigation?

Throughout the world, then, "encroachment" (used in a value-free sense) into low lying, flood-prone areas is a major factor enhancing flood risk. And everywhere the "levee effect" ensures that the economic cost of flood disasters will continue to increase.

Infrastructure developments for the tourist industry provide some of the most blatant examples of encroachment. A simple illustration is provided by the placement of campsites in shaded, riverside locations, where sudden-onset flood events may have disastrous consequences (see Figure 1). Such sites are deliberately located to take advantage of scenic attractiveness and to provide a wide range of leisure facilities for the tourist. The example illustrates a more widespread problem in tourist areas, namely that it is often the high-risk components of the landscape that are the most attractive from the tourist's point of view. High mountains, snow-capped in winter or throughout the year, attract skiers, walkers and general sightseers; deep valleys and steep gorges are focal points on scenic tours; and water, whether in river channels, lakes, or at the coast, plays a major role in both active and passive tourism.

This problem is often exacerbated by the attraction for tourists of landscapes on a much larger scale than they experience in their home areas. The appeal of "the big country" has been used to woo visitors to many areas, e.g. Africa, Australia, the United States. Unfamiliarity with the larger-scale landscape may reduce, rather than increase, perceptions of risk, especially for tourists travelling alone or in small family groups. Visitors to high mountain ranges, for example, may fail to comprehend either the present volume or the potential variability of streamflows. The Big Thompson canyon flood in July 1976 resulted from 300 mm of thunderstorm rainfall in less than six hours and drowned 139 people, many of them tourists unaware of the dangers of flash floods or of the need for urgent retreat from the canyon floor (Smith, 1992). Again, the valleys of major continental rivers are often so large as to be unrecognisable to visiting tourists who may not therefore be aware that they are at risk from flooding.

Perceptions of flood risks are also reduced in areas whose main attraction for tourists is the lack of rainfall. Intense convectional storms in such areas may be vary localised but the resulting floodwaves can move rapidly down dry channels into adjacent areas where no rain has fallen and where the visitor would not therefore expect flooding to occur. Moreover, in low rainfall areas, rivers and streams are ephemeral and often lack the clearly defined channels of perennial streams in wetter areas. Flood flows, when they occur, may not therefore always follow the same route down-valley and this increases further the risk that the tourist may be caught unaware. Very high flood risks are experienced by settlements built on alluvial fans, where water courses are mobile and velocities and sediment loads are high. Many resort and vacation towns in the desert areas of the south-western United States are located on alluvial fans, e.g. Desert Hot Springs in California, and represent disasters waiting to happen.

The development of tourism, and particularly the location of tourism plant and infrastructure, should always be predicated on the basis that low-rainfall areas are not no-rainfall areas and that dry river channels and valley bottoms may be suddenly and disastrously flooded. Yet there are many examples in low-rainfall areas of the indiscriminate development of tourism infrastructure, e.g. autoroutes, holiday apartments, etc., built across dry water courses with inadequate provision for the culverting and bypassing of floodwaters.

In many cases such examples reflect no more than cynical cost-cutting by developers more interested in maximising short-term gains than in protecting tourists against long-term risks. There are, however, tourist areas especially those in which "difficult" terrain (e.g. narrow valleys, coasts, etc.) is part of the attraction where the understandable wish to locate tourist facilities in close proximity to existing settlements almost inevitably means that the tourism plant has to be located at high-risk sites, simply because the existing, indigenous settlements have already occupied the few available "safe" sites.

Managing flood disasters in tourist areas

Smith (1992) summarised the three main hazard responses as modifying the burden of loss, modifying vulnerability to the flood event, and modifying the flood event itself. Loss modification may be achieved through action taken either before or after the event, e.g. through insurance programmes or disaster aid. Vulnerability modification is brought about largely by pre-event actions, e.g. development of community preparedness and of forecasting and warning schemes, and through legislation for appropriate land-use planning and building codes. Modification of the flood event depends on prior action, either in the river basin in order to reduce the amount of floodwater produced, or at the hazard site in order to reduce the impact of a given flood event.

A slightly different flood disaster terminology has been adopted by the United Nations Disaster Relief Organization (UNDRO) and the IDNDR (UNDRO, 1991). In this scheme "loss modification" is incorporated into a three-part post-disaster response involving *relief, rehabilitation* and *reconstruction.* "Vulnerability modification" is largely covered by the term *"preparedness",* and "event modification" by the unduly optimistic term *"prevention."* Both preparedness and prevention depend, for maximum effectiveness, on a third pre-disaster mitigation component, risk assessment.

This review of disaster management in tourist areas will concentrate on preparedness and prevention, with reference in each case to the appropriate aspect of risk assessment, i.e. vulnerability assessment in relation to preparedness, and flood hazard assessment in relation to prevention. As was discussed in the previous section, the discussion is predicated on the assumption that there is no specific "tourist area" response to flood disaster management, so that much of what follows will be of a general nature. This is not to deny that there are many individual "tourist" examples, such as the disaster emergency measures set out for National Parks and many of the urban tourist complexes in the United States.

Flood disaster preparedness

Flood disaster preparedness comprises the range of short-term or emergency measures which come into force when flood conditions threaten, and which remain in force during the flood event and for an appropriate period afterwards. Such measures will be fully effective only if there is a high level of community preparedness involving advanced planning by both institutions and individuals.

Effective flood disaster preparedness demands a high level of organisation and coordination and the clear definition and regular updating of the chains of responsibility and operational roles of the appropriate government ministries and agencies, e.g. those responsible for transport, public works, health, welfare, broadcasting and telephones, agriculture and meteorology and hydrology. It should also include the treasury in relation to emergency funding, and the National Red Cross Society and other similar bodies.

The appropriate degree of coordination might be achieved through the establishment of flood disaster-preparedness committees at the national and local level (ESCAP/WMO/LRCS, 1977), or through some other form of organisation. In either case the key functions to be performed would include the following:

(a)   Keeping the population prepared for a flood emergency;
(b)   Reviewing, and acting on, matters likely to reduce danger and damage from flooding;
(c)   Supervising warning systems and the organisations for dealing with emergencies;
(d)   Directing and controlling rescue and relief work;
(e)   Liaising with the media and organizing programmes of public information and education; and
(f)   Organizing post-event surveys of damage, injuries and deaths and taking action on the lessons to be learned.

Effective organisation implies that the requisite legislation for flood disaster-preparedness is in place. This should cover:

(a)   The monitoring of hydrometeorological conditions, the issue of warnings and the actions that should follow;
(b)   The conduct of emergency procedures such as flood fighting and evacuation;
(c)   The operation of systems for protection, rescue and relief;
(d)   The education and information of both the permanent and transient population;
(e)   The preservation of public health and social order;
(f)   The establishment of procedures for rehabilitation and restoration; and
(g)   The implementation of appropriate financial arrangements.

FLOOD SAFETY RULES

Before the flood
1.   Keep on hand materials like sandbags, plywood, plastic sheeting and lumber.
2.   Install check valves in building sewer traps, to prevent flood water from backing up in sewer drains.
3.   Arrange for auxiliary electrical supplies for hospitals and other operations which are critically affected by power failure.
4.   Keep first aid supplies at hand.
5.   Keep your automobile fueled; if electric power is cut off, filling stations may not be able to operate pumps for several days.
6.   Keep a stock of food which requires little cooking equipment, lights and flashlights in working order.

When you receive a flood warning
8.   Store drinking water in clean bathtubs, and in various containers; water service may be interrupted.
9.   If forced to leave your home and time permits, move essential items to save ground; fill tanks to keep them from floating; grease immovable machinery.
10. Move to a safe area before access is cut off by flood water.

During the flood
11   Avoid areas subject to sudden flooding.
12. Do not attempt to cross a flowing stream where water is above your knees.
13. Do not attempt to drive over a flooded road — you can be stranded and trapped.

After the flood
14. Do not eat fresh food that has come into contact with flood waters.
15. Test drinking water for potability; wells should be pumped out and the water tested before drinking.
16. Seek necessary medical care at the nearest hospital; food, clothing, shelter and first aid are available at Red Cross shelters.
17. Do not visit the disaster area; your presence might hamper rescue and other emergency operations.
18. Do not handle live electrical equipment in wet areas; electrical equipment should be checked and dried before returning to service.
19. Use flashlights, not lanterns or torches, to examine buildings; flammables may be inside.
20. Report broken utility lines to appropriate authorities.

FLASH FLOODS

Flash floods move at incredible speeds, can roll boulders, tear out trees, destroy buildings and bridges, and scour out new channels. Killing walls of water can reach 10 to 20 feet. You won't always have warning that these deadly, sudden floods are coming.
WHEN A FLASH FLOOD WARNING IS ISSUED FOR YOUR AREA OR THE MOMENT YOU FIRST REALIZE THAT A FLASH FLOOD IS IMMINENT, ACT QUICKLY TO SAVE YOURSELF. YOU MAY ONLY HAVE SECONDS.

Get out of areas subject to flooding. Avoid already flooded areas. Do not attempt to cross a flowing stream on foot where the water is above your knees. If driving, know the depth of the water in a dip before crossing. The road may not be intact under the water. If the vehicle stalls, abandon it immediately and seek higher ground - rapidly rising water may engulf the vehicle and its occupants and sweep them away. Be especially cautious at night when it is harder to recognize flood dangers.

DURING ANY FLOOD EMERGENCY, STAY TUNED TO YOUR RADIO OR TELEVISION STATION. INFORMATION FROM NOAA AND CIVIL EMERGENCY FORCES MAY SAVE YOUR LIFE.

Figure 2 — Flood safety rules published by NOAA.

It is important throughout to involve and cooperate with the general public and to recognise that the population in tourist areas is often more mobile and more transient than elsewhere. Effective involvement implies that the general public is educated about flood disaster preparedness and that information is regularly updated and repeated since, even for long-term residents, "living memory" has a duration of little more than seven years. Furthermore, in tourist areas there may be a need to provide for multilingual education and information-dissemination and to cooperate with the country of origin of tourists. The local school and college education programmes will be a relatively less important way of dissemination than, say, posters and other media displays. These should be widely broadcast and distributed, informative, and clearly and simply expressed. Maps showing flood-prone areas and evacuation routes from them are particularly important. Equally important are clearly stated flood safety rules, such as those published by the National Oceanographic and Atmosphere Agency (NOAA) in the United States, covering the periods before, during and after the flood event (see Figure 2).

Flood forecasts and warnings represent a fundamental component of flood disaster-preparedness. Accuracy is essential. A gross underestimate on a previous occasion may result in unnecessary worry or panic on the next occasion and previous overestimates may lead to complacency. Accurate forecasts and warnings need an efficient hydrometerological monitoring network, highly skilled forecasting personnel, and a rapid and robust system for disseminating the warnings to the appropriate official agencies and to the general public. Radio and television services are usually the surest way to reach most people. Again, it is important to emphasise possible language problems in relation to the dissemination of warnings to hoteliers and tourists and the special problems of locating and alerting mobile tourists such as campers and canoeists.

Once flood warnings have been received, various forms of emergency action, including flood fighting, flood proofing and evacuation, can be put into effect.

Flood fighting covers a number of pre-arranged and preferably well-rehearsed precautionary measures taken during flood events. Although advice and financial assistance will normally be provided by the central government, the organisation and implementation of flood fighting measures is essentially a community task which may be spearheaded by a specially trained flood-fighting corps (ESCAP/WMO/LRCS, 1977). Techniques include: rescheduling of reservoir operations in order to minimise downstream spillage during the period of maximum flood flows; the operation of flood-control gates, tidal barriers and locks; and the protection of flood embankments (or levees) against collapse, leakage or overflow by using straw mats, sandbags, etc.

Flood proofing involves a variety of adjustments to buildings and their contents intended to reduce flood losses (Smith 1992). While many of the measures involve permanent design changes (and should therefore properly be considered under the heading of "flood prevention"), some are temporary and can be activated on receipt of flood warning, e.g. blocking up apertures, sealing doors and windows, sandbagging, etc.

Evacuation of people, and property if time permits, is the ultimate response to major flood disasters and the only effective means of protecting against large-scale loss of life. It is therefore crucial to ensure the highest possible level of prior planning and the provision of accurate flood forecasts with long lead-times.

Even where the financial, transportational and other resources are readily available, evacuation is logistically demanding, highly disruptive, and commonly resisted vigorously by those at risk from inundation. In developing countries, where available resources are inadequate and the population of flood-prone areas is large, evacuation poses frequently insurmountable problems, with consequentially disastrous losses of life.

It is therefore of the greatest importance that evacuation plans are carefully based on assessments of vulnerability and that maps and diagrams are drawn and disseminated prioritising areas to be evacuated and showing the location of areas, places and buildings to be used as shelters, and the assembly points and routes to be used during the evacuation process given different flood warning lead-times and different predicted floodwater depths.

In order to remain fully effective, the planning and organisation of flood disaster preparedness needs to be subjected to regular review and testing. Ideally, this will involve regular meetings of the many agencies and individuals whose close cooperation during a flood disaster is absolutely crucial, and theoretical and practical exercises — including occasional full-scale mobilization — so that deficiencies in preparedness can be identified and rectified.

A high level of flood disaster preparedness, regularly reviewed and tested, should then mean that, when a flood disaster occurs, emergency operations, disaster relief and cooperation with the countries of origin of tourists caught in the flooding can proceed smoothly and effectively.

To assist resort managers, checklists covering emergency preparations, information for tourists and information for employees and their families are presented in Appendices A, B and C.

Flood disaster prevention

Although the term "flood prevention" is used in this section, it is an unduly optimistic one since, except for comparatively low-magnitude events, flooding and flood disasters cannot be "prevented." Once the flood risk has been fully assessed, however, the flood hazard may be *mitigated* by a number of measures intended to increase the level of permanent protection against inundation. In other words, there are other important responses to the flood hazard than "preparedness."

Clearly, the objectives of flood disaster prevention are to reduce the magnitude of flood disasters — especially in developing countries where such a high proportion of the population may be at risk — and thereby to reduce the reliance on relief and emergency measures during and after flood events. Flood disaster prevention measures are complex because of their wide scope and their technical content, and because they involve a consideration not just of flood disasters themselves, but also of interactions between development and the environment on one hand and between social and economic aims on the other (ESCAP/WMO/LRCS, 1977). Accordingly, flood disaster prevention should form an integral part of the national planing process. Broadly speaking, measures for flood disaster prevention fall into two types, i.e. structural and non-structural. Structural measures are normally more costly, often excessively so in relation to the national budgets of many developing countries. During IDNDR it will be important to ensure that superficially "glamorous" methods are not given undue preference over simpler, less expensive methods that are often equally effective.

Just as the adoption of flood disaster-preparedness measures should be based on vulnerability assessments, so the adoption of flood disaster-prevention measures should be preceded by proper flood hazard assessment and evaluation. Such evaluation is common practice in many countries and the importance of its wider adoption has been recognized by the World Meteorological Organization (WMO) and the United Nations Environment Programme (UNEP) in relation to river flooding and storm surge inundations resulting from tropical cyclones. Flood hazard assessment requires good hydrometeorological networks and long-term data as well as an appropriate scientific input to the analysis and interpretation of those data.

Another desirable prerequisite for flood-disaster prevention is a national programme of legislation covering appropriate areas such as land use, planning, building, civil engineering construction and public health. In some cases such legislation will complement existing legislation for other purposes: in relation to river basin and flood-plain management the likely complementarity between legislation for environmental protection and legislation for flood mitigation is obvious. Equally obvious is that legislation for flood mitigation purposes may interact much less harmoniously with, say, social legislation. It is thus important to ensure that legislation for flood disaster-prevention should not negate the goals of social and economic development in tourist areas, e.g. through unduly restrictive zoning and building codes.

Structural measures. A wide range of engineering structures permits a degree of flood control, either by containing floodwaters within a flood-prone area, e.g. within embankments or enlarged channels, or by reducing the flow of floodwater through the area, e.g. by the use of diversion channels or upstream reservoir storage. None of these methods completely prevents flooding. To be effective against the largest floods, both their size and cost would be prohibitive and their adverse effects on landscape aesthetics, especially in tourist areas, would be totally unacceptable. They can provide protection up to a design limit, however, and that design limit is normally greater in urban than in rural areas.

Embankments (also called dykes, levees, bunds and stopbanks) are the most common and usually the least expensive type of flood control structure. For millennia they have been constructed by riverine and coastal communities and individuals to protect their holdings. Many thousands of kilometres of embankments have been built in China, the Indian subcontinent and the United States.

In the case of river floods, embanking is often combined with either channel enlargement, which increases the flood-carrying capacity of the channel, or with the construction of diversion channels.

Reservoirs too have been used for thousands of years to ameliorate the effects of flooding, by storing floodwater behind dams so that it can subsequently be released downstream in a controlled way. However, protection against large floods requires large and expensive dams and in some countries the volumes of floodwater generated are so large that reservoir storage is simply not a practical option for flood amelioration. For example, it would take some 66 billion m3 of reservoir storage (more than 1700 Lake Meads!) to make a significant impact on major floods in Bangladesh (Rogers et al., 1989). Reservoirs in tourist areas, particularly those developed for their warmth and dryness, have often added substantially to the attractiveness and recreational resources of such areas, e.g. the reservoirs on the Colorado River system in the United States.

However effective flood control may be, inundation of flood-prone land will always occur, given a sufficiently rare event. In such cases the scale of disaster impact may be significantly reduced if proper building codes, designed to combat the effects of floods, have been adopted and implemented. Flood-proofing measures were outlined by Hoyt and Langbein (1955) and specified in detail by Sheffer (1960) as "permanent," "contingent" or "emergency" measures. The main considerations to be addressed were summarized in ESCAP/WMO/LRCS (1977) as follows:

(a) Proper anchorage to prevent buildings floating away from their foundations;

(b) Adequate elevation of basement and first (i.e. ground) floors;

(c) Sufficient strength to withstand the pressure of fast-moving water;

(d) Avoidance of building materials which deteriorate rapidly when exposed to water; and

(e) Prohibited installation of items and materials (e.g. unprotected electrical equipment, chemical materials, etc.) which are hazardous when submerged.

In respect to tourist plant, such as hotels, the appropriate flood-proofing would ensure that essential services, including food service, and all guest rooms were located above flood level.

Non-structural measures. Land-use planning and zoning in flood plains and in coastal areas prone to inundation are widely used, and even more widely advocated, as a means of reducing flood hazards. In many countries planning legislation clearly enforces zoning and other regulations for controlling both the type of land use and also the density and pace of development. In the case of river flood plains this may result in a designated "floodway" adjacent to the channel, in which no building or landfill is allowed, beyond which is a "floodway fringe," where development may be permitted subject to being protected, e.g. by fill or flood proofing. A third zone extends to the outer limits of some defined major flood (e.g. the Standard Project Flood in the United States) and will remain unflooded in most years so that a greater complexity of land use and development may be permitted. Similar regulatory structures may be applied to flood-prone coastal areas.

Land-use regulation and zoning for controlling tourism development should be applied whenever possible. Although appropriate for many kinds of development, e.g. hotels, it is more difficult to apply in the general sense that it is often those parts of the landscape which are most at risk from flooding that are most attractive to tourists. Particular care must be taken in this case to minimize the flood disaster-risk in other ways.

Financial measures may be used to supplement land-use controls in order to limit encroachment. These may take the form either of weighted insurance premiums or a variety of taxation measures intended to encourage development away from flood-prone areas, or of government action to acquire flood-prone land by compulsory purchase order. In the latter case, additional tourism and recreational benefits may be derived, e.g. the creation of public parkland, wetland conservation, improved access to waterside land, etc. (Handmer, 1987).

Another non-structural approach is that of flood hazard abatement, or catchment management, where action is taken in the catchment upstream of the flood hazard area in order to reduce the volume and discharge of flood-waters generated by rainfall or meltwater. Such action may involve changing the land use and vegetation cover (e.g. afforestation), modifying agricultural practices in order to reduce rapid run-off and soil erosion, managing forested areas in order to prolong the period of snowmelt and thereby reduce flood peaks, or modifying surface and drainage properties in urban areas. Such measures may cause a significant amelioration of smaller flood peaks, but will have little or no impact on the rarer, high magnitude events. However, action to prevent catchment degradation should always be encouraged.

In respect of tourist plant, such as hotels, the appropriate flood-proofing would ensure that essential services — including food service — and all guest rooms were located above floor level.

CHAPTER IV

EARTHQUAKES AND TOURISM

Introduction

During this century earthquakes have caused loss of life in at least 50 countries, with more than 1.5 million known fatalities arising from 1150 events (Coburn and Spence. 1992). Many earthquake-prone areas are also popular tourist resorts; they include the Mediterranean, the Middle East, Southeast Asia, China, Japan, the Pacific coast of the Americas, the Caribbean, New Zealand and the Pacific Islands. Tour operators are confused about the earthquake dangers in these places, and need to be given accurate and helpful advice so they are neither unduly alarmed nor lulled into a false sense of security. In more developed areas, such as California and Japan, there will be well enforced anti-earthquake regulations and emergency procedures, and local authorities will provide adequate guidance. In some other areas, however, local guidance and control will be minimal, and those with responsibility for tourist facilities will need to take expert advice from elsewhere.

Much fear of earthquakes stems from ignorance, but with sound advice and proper planning and precautions, the earthquake threat can be reduced to acceptable levels and need not inhibit tourist activity.

Earthquakes and their occurrence

What are earthquakes?

Earthquakes are among the most terrifying of natural phenomena. Much of this fear comes from lack of simple knowledge of what earthquakes are and what effects they can produce. To the scientist an earthquake is a sudden rupture in the rock beneath the Earth's surface, from which elastic vibrations spread out. When these reach the surface they may be felt as earthquake shaking and, if severe enough, cause destructive effects. The "size" of the earthquake, that is its magnitude on the Richter scale, is a measure of the total energy released at the source. This is a logarithmic scale, with each step of one magnitude meaning that the ground shakes 10 times as much and the energy released increases 30 fold.

The effects of an earthquake are described by its intensity on the Modified-Mercalli scale. The severity of shaking at any particular place, that is, the earthquake's intensity there, will depend on how big the earthquake is (its magnitude), how far away it is, the type of soil, and for buildings, the type and standard of construction. Because of these factors, the biggest earthquakes are not necessarily those that cause the most damage or attract the most publicity. For instance, the biggest earthquake in the world in the last 20 years years took place on the Macquarie Ridge between New Zealand and the Antarctic in May 1989. Despite its magnitude of 8.3, its remoteness from land meant that it was hardly reported by the popular media. At the other end of the scale, the Agadir earthquake of 1960, which killed about 12 000 people in Morocco through the collapse of buildings, was of a magnitude less than 6, as was the earthquake at Cairo in October 1992, which resulted in more than 400 deaths. The Tangshan earthquake in China in 1976 was an example of a large event (magnitude 7.8) close to a major city, where the collapse of poor buildings resulted in at least 240 000 deaths. The effects of the type of ground were dramatically demonstrated in Mexico City in 1985, when vibrations from a large earthquake 300 km away were greatly increased by soft sediments under the city, resulting in about 10 000 deaths. It was this same effect of soft soil which caused the collapse of the freeway at Oakland, 100 km away from the centre of the Californian earthquake of October 1989.

Where do earthquakes occur?

Most earthquakes take place along certain well defined zones which mark the boundaries between rigid blocks, or "plates" which extend for at least 100 km into the Earth. The most active of these boundaries of "interplate" earthquakes is along the western side of the Pacific Ocean from the Aleutian Islands through Japan, the Philippines, Indonesia and the South Pacific to the south of New Zealand. This area experiences about 85 per cent of the world's earthquakes. Other active plate boundaries run down the eastern side of the Pacific (e.g. California, Mexico and Chile), and from the Mediterranean. Other plate boundaries pass through the middle of deep oceans, resulting in earthquakes being experienced on islands such as Iceland and the Azores.

It is wrong, however, to think that all earthquakes happen on plate boundaries. Many occur inside plates, such as the small and moderate sized events in northern Europe, but these "interplate" earthquakes can be very large, such as those in the central United States in 1812 and the Tangshan earthquake of 1976. Because intraplate earthquakes are not as frequent as those on plate boundaries and are scattered more widely, they tend to occur at places where few anti-earthquake precautions have been taken, and their effects can be much more severe than would be expected from earthquakes of similar size in more active areas.

How often do earthquakes occur?

People are often surprised by the number of earthquakes detected by the major seismological agencies. For instance, the International Seismological Centre in England lists about 3 000 earthquakes a month worldwide, that is about one every 15 minutes. Most of these are far too small to be felt, and are recorded only by instruments. There is about one magnitude 8 earthquake a year somewhere in the world, and for each drop of one magnitude the number increases roughly 10-fold, so we expect about one magnitude 7 earthquake a month, and two a week of magnitude 6, the size of the damaging earthquake in Cairo in 1992.

What can be done to reduce earthquake effects?

We cannot prevent earthquakes, but much can be done to lessen their effects. Prediction in the popular sense is not yet possible, is never likely to be accurate and is not the answer. Rather than trying to predict individual earthquakes, seismologists now aim to determine earthquake "hazard", that is, the likelihood of shaking of a given severity at a given place, taking account of the distribution of earthquakes and local ground conditions.

The first step is land-use planning. Areas of poor ground, or near faults that might move should not be used for high-occupancy buildings such as halls, places of worship, schools or hotels. Appropriate building regulations

must be formulated and enforced for new construction, and existing structures evaluated and, if need be, strengthened or demolished. A few simple
criteria in design can make buildings much more safe. Many national
agencies give such advice. Buildings should be simple in form, and preferably symmetric and free from overhanging parapets and awnings that could
fall on passers-by. Walls should be well braced with architectural features
such as an open lower story for ventilation or parking avoided. Simple
precautions inside buildings can also reduce damage and casualties. Portable
heaters and heavy furniture should be secured and cupboard doors bolted.
Planning for earthquakes includes keeping emergency equipment and
supplies in a safe place, as well as having household, institutional and
community plans for action in the event of a serious earthquake.

During an earthquake the most important thing is not to rush outside,
where there could be great danger from falling masonry and collapsing structures. Strong shaking rarely lasts more than 30 seconds to one minute,
although it might seem longer! During this time people should seek shelter in
some protected place like a doorway or under a desk or table. They should
only leave a building, in an orderly manner, once the strong shaking has
stopped. People caught outside should move away from structures that might
fall on them, and avoid obvious dangers such as broken power lines. In steep
areas the earthquake might trigger landslides, but the ground does not open
up and swallow people.

Immediately after a severe earthquake the risk of fire must be reduced
by turning off electric and gas supplies, and ensuring that no naked flames
are burning. Casualties must be attended to and moved to places of safety.
There is likely to be loss of services such as electricity, gas and telephone.
Sewage pipes are likely to be broken and water supply lost or contaminated.

Another disturbing factor is the occurrence of aftershocks which
aggravate damage in structures already affected. Aftershocks seldom reach
the severity of the main shock, but they can have disturbing psychological
effect on survivors, and also on relief workers when night time shocks
interfere with sleep. Aftershock sequences can last for days or weeks, and
although the interval between individual shocks should lengthen, large
aftershocks can occur late in the sequence, as well as soon after the main
event.

Effects on tourism
Comparison with other hazards
Although large earthquakes make spectacular news coverage, the overall risk
from earthquakes remains negligible compared with those from other sources.
In California, for example, the total number of deaths from all earthquakes since
European settlement is about 800, the same number of people killed on California
roads every six months, and an even larger number die from smoking-related
diseases. The worst-affected buildings are usually structures of the poorest quality, while tourist hotels are often among the better engineered buildings.

Earthquakes are not the only natural hazard to threaten tourists. In many
places wind storms are a regular occurrence, and share many common features
with earthquakes. In Hong Kong, for instance, buildings designed to withstand the
strong winds incorporate much anti-seismic resistance. Civil defence plans such
as those specifically developed in Florida for hurricanes also have many appli-

cations for earthquake preparedness and relief. One big difference is that wind storms are often preceded by some warning; earthquakes are not.

One earthquake-related hazard which must be taken seriously is the tsunami, or sea seismic wave. Certain types of marine earthquake can generate waves on the sea surface, and local shorelines can modify the waves so that water recedes and advances with devastating effect. A particular danger is when the water recedes first and sightseers and gatherers of sea life move onto beaches, only to be overwhelmed by the returning onrush of water. Potential tsunamis can travel as small waves with the speed of jet aircraft for large distances across deep oceans, to increase many-fold in size when they come to islands or steep shore lines. Thus the great Chilean earthquake of 1960 caused tsunami damage in Hawaii, and in 1992 two catastrophic tsunamis killed over 2 000 people. The particular mechanism of an earthquake in Nicaragua in September resulted in a much larger tsunami than might have been expected from its magnitude, while another earthquake in Indonesia in December resulted in a wave up to 26 metres in height which completely destroyed villages on the island of Flores.

People near beaches and low-lying land in tsunami-prone areas should have it impressed on them always to seek higher ground following a severe earthquake and never to approach the beach. Hawaii and many other places in the Pacific belong to a "tsunami warning system" which may give warning of an impending tsunami following a major earthquake. Any such warnings should be taken extremely seriously.

Even in active earthquake areas, the risk to tourists from earthquakes is not unduly large compared with other risks associated with travelling, including other natural hazards, transport accidents and crime. Nevertheless, there is action which the tourist industry can take to lessen the risk of its customers being affected by earthquakes, and to reassure them.

Public information

In general, with publicity and in response to specific enquiries, it is best to treat earthquakes in a matter-of-fact manner. If a tourist area such as Greece is known for earthquakes, this should not be hidden, and any enquiries should be met with reassurance about the standard of construction and level of precautions. It should be remembered that in areas where earthquakes have occurred in the past, most existing buildings will have already experienced shaking and survived. Resort managers should include copies of pages B-5 and B-6 as part of standard welcome packages provided in guest rooms. These pages provide immediate guidance to tourists in the event of an earthquake. Information specific to the hotel should be included as well.

In the time immediately following a major earthquake, people will ask if there will be more. This is always difficult to answer, as some aftershocks must be expected and, although it is not usual for these to approach the strength of the main shock, there is always a slight possibility of this. Communications may be a problem. Tourism agencies should have means of keeping in touch with their main hotels, preferably by mains-independent radio to establish the safety of their customers. If there is a breakdown of civil amenities, particularly water and power supplies, or where there is a risk of disease, tourists should be evacuated from the affected areas.

Apart from those in earthquake-affected areas, there will be relatives at home and other who have already booked to go to the area who will need reassuring. As long as the facilities are unaffected, there is no reason why normal tourism activity should not continue. At such times, the advice of a major seismological agency can be helpful. The public may also confuse geographic areas. For instance, in large countries such as Indonesia or the Philippines, an earthquake at one end of the country will have no bearing on tourism activities many hundreds or even thousands of kilometres away in the same country.

A related problem is when there are media reports of earthquake prediction. These are notoriously difficult to deal with. Many reported predictions, sometimes quite specific, come from non-specialists and can be discounted by the reputable scientific bodies. In these cases, however, the normal probability of earthquakes is not affected, and the prediction could be fulfilled by chance. When discussing a dubious prediction, it is best not to say that an earthquake will not take place, but rather that the chances of an earthquake occurring are no different from usual. Up to now, the only successful scientific prediction of a major earthquake was that in north China in 1975, when the population of the town Haicheng was moved outdoors several hours before an earthquake of magnitude 7.3. Since then, no prediction of significance has been achieved, although some major seismological agencies, especially in California and Japan, are carrying out extensive monitoring. Warnings issued by these agencies should be taken seriously, and specialist advice sought.

Dealing with an earthquake threat before the event
Selecting sites for tourist facilities

The first step is to establish the overall level of earthquake hazard in the area. If the country has a specialized seismological agency, this should be consulted. If no such agency exists, or if a broader picture is desired, information can be obtained from an international agency (e.g. the International Seismological Centre, England, or the U.S. National Earthquake Center). Some insurance organisations also provide such information, and in particular Munich Reinsurance publishes a World Map of Natural Hazards, with an accompanying explanatory booklet. The Swiss Reinsurance Company also publishes booklets on individual earthquakes and hazard assessment. A list of organisations providing information on earthquakes is given in Table 1.

Such generalized hazard assessment will give background information for an area, but this must be extended to take account of individual site conditions arising from steepness of ground, soil conditions relative to amplification of vibration and liquefaction potential, and closeness to tectonic features such as activity faults. In tsunami-prone areas seafront-sites should be carefully assessed. If no local advice is available, specialized engineering geologists should be consulted.

Buildings and structures

Any local building regulations must be complied with for both new and existing structures. Tourist authorities and operators should satisfy themselves that these regulations are met, and if in doubt consult earthquake specialist engineers. National building regulations are compiled in *Earthquake Resistant Regulations: A World List* issued by the International Association for Earthquake Engineering (IAEE). The 1988 edition lists reg-

Table 1
Organizations conducting research into earthquakes

Agencies	Publications
International Association for Earthquake Engineering (IAEE) Kenchiku Kaikan, 3rd Floor 5-26-20 Shiba Minato-ku Tokyo, 108 Japan	*Earthquake Regulations: A World List,* 1988
International Conference Building Officials (ICBO) Whittier, CA, USA	*The Uniform Building Code,* 1988
International Seismological Centre (ISC) Pipers Lane, Thatcham Newbury RG13 4NS, UK	*Regional Catalogue of Earthquakes* (biannual) *Felt and Damaging Earthquakes* (annual)
National Center for Earthquake Engineering Research (NCEER) State University of New York Red Jacket Quadrangle, Box 610025 Buffalo, NY, USA	Quarterly bulletins
National Earthquake Information Center (NEIC) US Geological Survey Denver Federal Center PO Box 25046, Mail Stop 967 Denver, CO, USA	Monthly listings of earthquakes
United Nations Disaster Relief Organization (UNDRO) Palais des Nations Geneva 10, CH-1211 Switzerland	*Mitigating Natural Disasters: Effects and Options,* 1

Commercial Organizations	Publications
Munich Reinsurance Company Königinstrasse 107 D-8000 Munich 40, Germany	*World Map of Natural Hazards,* 1988 Studies of specific earthquakes
Swiss Reinsurance Company Mythenquai 50/60 CH-8022 Zurich, Switzerland	*A Short Guide to Earthquake Risk Assessment,* 1977 Studies of specific earthquakes

ulations from 36 countries. If the country concerned is not listed, a useful alternative is provided by the Uniform Building Code published for the United States (ICBO), with regulations specified for zones of four different degrees of hazard. Reference to a map such as that of Munich Reinsurance may be used to determine the appropriate zone. A new "Eurocode" is being developed to standardize requirements in the European Union, but is several years from completion.

In a few countries authorities require buildings older than a certain age to be modified to meet current requirements. This may involve substantial cost. Any existing tourist facility in an earthquake-prone country should be periodically inspected by a competent earthquake engineer.

As well as the main structure, attention should be paid to interior fittings, such as loose ceiling tiles, that could fall and injure occupants, and to heavy external ornamentation that could fall on passers-by and people leaving the building. Exits should be clearly marked and able to be opened at all times, as for fire precautions. This is especially important when the type of construction is such that fire is likely to follow an earthquake. Emergency equipment should be prominently available. In Japan, for example, hotels have fire buckets, ropes, ladders and axes in corridors. There should be an emergency lighting system independent of the main supply.

Emergency planning and information for hotel guests
In many parts of the world where earthquakes occur, local authorities will have plans with advice on preparedness before the event, and on action to take during and after an earthquake. In particular, California, Japan and New Zealand are well organized in this respect, and local information should be available to guide hotel operators. In some of these countries relevant information is included in telephone directories or on their covers.

If no such information is available, the management of tourist facilities should compile suitable information notices to be prominently displayed in public places and private rooms, and possibly included in hotel television programmes. In these, earthquake precautions should be given similar prominence to fire precautions and there should be clear instructions on what to do in the case of earthquake or fire, including evacuation plans. Mock earthquake drills similar to fire drills should be held periodically.

Given the likelihood that earthquakes will occur, it is essential that all tourist establishments have a clear emergency plan with well-defined responsibilities allocated to duty staff, on a position basis rather than to individuals. These responsibilities should include reassuring guests during the event, checking for casualties afterwards, supervising any necessary evacuation of premises and guiding guests to a pre-arranged place of safety.

Coping during the event
Earthquake shaking does not last long. During this time staff and those in authority must remain calm and reassure others. They should actively discourage any rush to exits, but advise people to move away from hazards — such as large areas of glass or tall unstable furniture — and to take shelter in places of local strength such as doorways and beneath tables.

Immediately after the event

Again the main responsibility of the staff is to remain calm and reassure guests. Local staff are likely to have experienced earthquakes before, but should remember that for many guests it is probably their first experience. If the shaking is only minor guests should be encouraged to carry on normally, but if it is severe guests should be guided outside. Casualties must be located, given first aid where appropriate and if possible moved to places of safety until specialized medical assistance is available. Efforts must be made to check hotel registers and guest lists to establish that all guests are accounted for. Specialized help should be sought for anyone trapped.

Services such as gas and electricity should be turned off and not used until established as safe. Once it is safe to do so, premises should be checked for the possibility of further damage through fire, water or other hazards.

After the event

The first response after an earthquake should be to the immediate safety of guests and employees. In the event of a major earthquake, an organizing point outdoors should be established and announced immediately. Regardless of the severity of the quake, the next most important action is inspection of the facilities for injured people and dangerous conditions. Appendix A provides a checksheet that can be used to initiate responses to the event. Included is guidance on inspections, utility cut-off, building clean-up, communications, guest and employee rosters, evacuation coordination, travel assistance and security coordination. Employees and their families will also need guidance on how to respond to these events. Appendix C, pages 102 and 103, should be provided to all employees in earthquake prone regions, and reissued in the event of an earthquake.

In addition to checks on gas and electricity supplies, it may be necessary to check that the water supply is uncontaminated and the sewage system unaffected.

If there is any doubt about the safety of the structure, buildings should not be re-occupied until a structural survey has been carried out by a qualified engineer. If repairs or strengthening are deemed necessary, the opportunity should be taken to bring the structure up to the standard required to comply with anti-seismic regulations.

Summary

Fortunately, major earthquakes are rare occurrences and although their effects can be catastrophic over restricted areas, the overall risk is not large compared with other hazards arising from travel. Sensible precautions in siting and in ensuring standards in design and construction can greatly reduce the risk of injury and damage in earthquake-prone areas.

Tourist facilities in earthquake regions should have adequate emergency plans and equipment, and information regarding these must be brought to the attention of those at risk. In the event of a major earthquake, or the prediction of one, advice should be sought from a competent seismological agency.

The possibility of earthquakes should not be hidden from prospective tourists, but reassurances given as to the reality of the risk.

CHAPTER V

AVALANCHES AND TOURISM

Introduction

Avalanches are of importance in all mountainous areas of the world, where a large proportion of precipitation falls as snow and where people are living or spending their leisure time under or on steep mountain slopes.

Many avalanche-prone areas are popular tourist resorts, for example the Alps, the Rocky Mountains and the Himalayas. As a result of the increasing number of people exposed to danger in these areas, mostly tourists on winter sports holidays, avalanche warning and avalanche control have become vitally important.

Between 1972-73 and 1991-92, 28 people per year were killed by avalanches in Switzerland on average with damage of about SwF60 million caused to infrastructures. Some 31 people per year have been killed in France and 13 in the United States during the same 20-year period. The winter of 1991-92 was catastrophic in Turkey, with 328 victims. Besides killed and injured people there is an enormous toll on houses, shelters, roads, high-tension lines and forests.

In more crowded and developed areas, such as the Alps, the avalanche control procedures, like avalanche forecasts, emergency measures and prevention information, are well established. In developing areas, such as the Himalayas, there is only minimal avalanche control; so tourists should always use a guide for winter sport activity and mountain climbing unless they are experts. Increasing pressure on land resources, leading to deforestation, may increase the avalanche risk in these areas.

Many avalanche problems arise from ignorance. With proper planning and precautions the avalanche threat can be reduced by an acceptable level of restriction on tourist activities.

The nature and causes of avalanches

An avalanche is a certain amount of fast moving snow. The form and size of starting zone, avalanche path and zone of deposit can vary widely. For the scope of this discussion two types of avalanches are distinguished:

(a) A "valley avalanche" or "catastrophic avalanche" breaking from high up can bury human beings in settled areas and result in enormous material damage. In more developed countries avalanche control (defence constructions and artificial release of avalanches and warning systems) have reduced the number of victims of this type of avalanche.

(b) A "touristic avalanche" can surprise a skier or a mountain climber who generally triggers the fatal avalanche himself or herself. It is estimated that in the Alps more than 80 per cent of all avalanche victims are skiers, snowboarders and winter climbers.

For an avalanche to occur there are four basic conditions: (1) accumulation of a critical mass of snow; (2) structural changes within the snow cover that reduce its mechanical stability; (3) a steep gradient which permits a gravity flow; and (4) an avalanche triggering mechanism (e.g. skiers). Avalanches descend most often during the winter; however, they can occur in high mountains at any time of the year.

The stability of the snow cover is the important factor in the release and characteristic features of avalanches. The weight of the snow cover exerts shear forces between the different layers of the snow pack. The avalanche starts spontaneously or with additional stress, for example the weight of a skier. It can also be triggered by fallen rock, ice and cornice. In a steep snow covered mountain area hundreds of avalanches can descend during a storm period. Mostly they are of little significance and cause no damage if no people or buildings are within their range.

The quantity and quality of snow cover is dependent on terrain, weather and climate. Terrain and weather conditions can change locally. A given snow mass may accumulate or diminish within a short time, or it can change its physical parameters. This is highly noticeable in springtime, when rising temperatures increase the avalanche danger level, especially in the afternoon. Because of the variety and complexity of the various avalanche-triggering parameters, even experts are not able to predict the fracturing of the snow cover and the formation of an avalanche on an individual slope. They can forecast, however, the probability of avalanche occurrence for a given area, without the exact moment of release. The probability of avalanche occurrence within a given area and given time frame is also called avalanche danger. It has to be distinguished from avalanche risk, which also includes the number of people and the value of infrastructure and settlements, etc. exposed to this danger.

A low avalanche danger level indicates that only small avalanches can be triggered on a few, very steep slopes with low stability of snow cover. A high avalanche danger level indicates that large avalanches can be triggered on steep slopes of all aspects and within a wide range of altitudes. Accurate avalanche forecasts need a snow, avalanche and weather monitoring network, expert knowledge and a system for the rapid communication of warnings to official agencies and the general public. To reach a large number of people avalanche bulletins are disseminated through radio, television, newspapers and telephone. In an emergency, radio and television are the fastest and safest ways to reach the public.

Valley avalanches
Effects of valley avalanches
During heavy snowfalls on unstable, old snow cover, large avalanches can occur and travel at high speeds for long distances. The resulting impact pressure on obstacles within the avalanche path is significant. Such impact pressure, and the air pressure related to powder avalanches, are capable of destroying strong structures. Existing settlements in the run-out zone of the avalanches, highways, railway lines, high-tension lines and other infrastructures are all endangered. Avalanche damage cannot entirely be avoided. Great attention is drawn to long-term avalanche protection measures like par-avalanche constructions, guidance dams, strengthening of settlements, etc.

Practical steps to deal with valley avalanches
Long-term avalanche protection measures must diminish the avalanche risk. Such measures are:

(a) Avalanche zoning: designation of endangered zones with prohibited or limited construction possibilities. The size of the zones will be dominated by the avalanche run-out distance, which is related to the size of the starting zone and the thickness of a triggered layer.

(b) Afforestation: this is the best and cheapest protection so forests above endangered areas should be protected and carefully maintained. A dense forest can prevent avalanches starting. Existing openings in an avalanche protection forest should be afforested. Temporary wooden paravalanche constructions should take over the supporting function until the trees are strong enough to prevent avalanches starting.

Avalanches starting above the treeline can only be prevented with permanent paravalanche constructions, e.g. snow bridges or snow nets made of steel. These structures support the snow cover and allow very little snow movement. Because of the high cost of such structures, a cost-benefit analysis is recommended which should also include the possibility of structures in the run-out zones (retaining and deflection walls, splitting wedges, galleries and tunnels over endangered roads or railways, etc.).

Even with the best of paravalanche construction measures, avalanches will still sometimes reach settled areas and endanger people. To reduce the risk of loss of life, avalanche warning — including the monitoring of known avalanche tracks — is also of great importance. It is based on physical and expert knowledge of weather and snow cover, on practical knowledge and on local snow and weather data.

For a well-organized local avalanche service it is then possible to react appropriately to hazardous situations. Possible actions include triggering avalanches artificially with explosives before their potential to harm becomes too high, closing roads, evacuating people from endangered areas and broadcasting information on how to behave. If evacuation is compulsory or if populated areas are inaccessible, food and water supplies are most important. It is possible to minimize avalanche damage with long-term avalanche protection measures and additionally to reduce negative effects with short-term measures. However, evacuation of people can sometimes be the only effective means of protection against loss of life in an emergency situation.

When a valley avalanche causes an emergency in populated areas, a team of professionals — politicians, ski-patrollers, physicians, the police, fire-brigade, military and civil rescue organisations, etc. must work together.

Tourist avalanches
Effects of tourist avalanches
Tourist avalanches are mostly small- or medium-sized avalanches, often triggered by skiing or other mountaineering activities.

More and more people are learning to ski and snowboard. On groomed, marked and controlled slopes the artificial triggering of avalanches with explosives and the closing of ski pistes are optimal means of reducing avalanche danger. In recent winters there have been very few avalanche victims on ski runs in the Alps. However, tourist resorts attract an increasing number of people who lack the knowledge and experience to behave appropriately in mountainous areas. Powder snow skiing beside marked pistes is becoming more and more attractive. The avalanche risk in tourist areas is therefore increasing.

About 10 per cent of those completely covered by snow are dead by the time the avalanche stops. They are killed by mechanical impacts. Half an hour later only about five out of 10 completely covered victims can be rescued alive. The cause of death is mostly asphyxia. One hour after an avalanche has occurred about three out of 10 victims are still alive. In this interval hyperthermia tends to be the cause of death. An avalanche is therefore always a threat to life and it is often too late to rescue somebody alive if help has to be requested. Nevertheless, all means to rescue victims should be taken. In many developed areas, mountain and air rescue organisations and avalanche dog teams exist. Many people carried along with avalanches are not completely covered, so observation of descent, and searching, even without the use of electronic devices, can save lives.

Practical steps to deal with tourist avalanches
Winter tourists should know the principles of how to avoid avalanche accidents. Three sources of information are of particular importance:
(a) Signs and barriers that indicate avalanche danger outside the secured and controlled ski runs.
(b) Avalanche warning bulletins, which are available in many mountain areas. These bulletins normally provide information on the probability of avalanches occurring in a certain areas with indications of altitude, exposition and steepness of hazardous slopes. They cannot forecast avalanches on individual slopes. In European countries the avalanche danger scale has been unified since winter 1993-94 (see Table 1).
(c) With a basic knowledge of various natural conditions resulting in avalanche danger, and with the experience of different techniques it is possible to estimate the avalanche risk of an individual slope (snow profile and Rutschblock anti-skid block).
This information helps winter climbers, hikers and skiers to plan a mountaineering tour and to estimate the safety of a given itinerary. Planning a mountain climb can be done in three steps:
(a) At home: getting weather and avalanche forecasts; finding a safe route with a map and guidebook; knowing how many experienced or inexperienced companions are participating, and their physical condition.
(b) Local: observing the snow-cover and especially the newly fallen snow, previous avalanches and actual weather situation (wind, glare, temperature and precipitation); watching the terrain (steepness, layout, vegetation and orography).
(c) before stepping onto a potentially unsafe slope: checking the danger level of the slope (e.g. testing the snowcover with the Rutschblock technique).
Those who only have minor knowledge of avalanches should leave marked trails only when the danger level is low. To get the necessary experience, tourists can join courses and guided tours led by mountain guides and experts. Unfortunately, most skiers and a lot of climbers do not see the need to get information and experience. Most of the new category of avalanche victims, the snowmobilers in North America, are particularly unaware of avalanche potential. National agencies providing research and information on avalanches are presented in Table 2.

Table 1
European avalanche risk scale

Degree of risk	Snowpack stability	Avalanche probability	Effects of traffic lines and residential area recommendations	Effects on off-piste skiers/recommendations
1. Low	The snowpack is generally well bonded and stable.	Likely to be triggered off by high additional loads[b] on only a very few extremely steep slopes.[d] Only small spontaneous avalanches (slushes) possible.	No risk of avalanches.	Virtually no restrictions for back-country and down hill skiing.
2. Moderate	The snowpack is moderately well bonded on some[a] steep slopes,[c] otherwise generally well bonded.	Likely to be triggered off by high additional loads, mainly on the steep slopes indicated. Large spontaneous avalanches not expected.	Virtually no risk of avalanches.	Often good conditions. Routes should be selected with care, especially on steep slopes in the direction[d] and altitude indicated.
3. Considerable	The snow pack is moderately to poorly bonded on many[a] steep slopes.	Likely to be triggered off by low additional loads[b] mainly on the steep slopes indicated. In some cases, mostly medium-sized and occasionally large spontaneous avalanches possible.	Traffic lines and individual buildings in risk areas endangered in exceptional cases. Precautionary steps should betaken when undertaking safety measures in these areas.	Back-country and downhill skiing should only be done by experienced people with good avalanche assessment abilities. Steep slopes in the directions and altitudes indicated should be avoided.
4. High	The snowpack is poorly bonded in most[a] places.	Likely to be triggered off even by low additional loads on most steep slopes. In some cases, many medium-sized and also large spontaneous avalanches expected.	This type of avalanche is usually spread over a wide area. Traffic lines and transport facilities in risk areas should occasionally be closed.	Back-country and downhill skiing should be restricted to moderately steep slopes; the foot of the slope may also be at risk.
5. Very high	The snowpack is generally poorly bonded and largely unstable.	Numerous large spontaneous avalanches expected, also in moderately steep terrain.	Extensive safety measures (closing facilities, evacuation) necessary.	No back-country and downhill skiing to be undertaken.

Notes:

a. generally described in more detail in the avalanche situation report (e.g. altitude, direction, type of terrain, etc.).
b. additional load: high: e.g. group of skiers, piste vehicle, avalanche detonation; low: e.g. skier, walker.
c. steep slopes: slopes with an incline of more than about 30°.
d. extremely steep slope: particularly unfavourable in terms of the incline, terrain, proximity to ridges. Direction: direction in which slope falls.

TABLE 2
National agencies conducting research into avalanches

Country	Agency
Austria	Institut für Lawinenkunde Hoftberg-Rennweg 1 6020 Innsbruck
France	Association Nationale pour L'Etude de la Neige et des Avalanches (ANENA) 5 rue Ernest Calvat 38000 Grenoble
	Centre D'Etude de la Neige Grenoble (CEN) Domaine Universitaire Boite Postale 44 38402 St. Martin d'Hères
Italy	Associazione Interregionale di Coordinamento e Documentazione per i Problemi Inerenti all Neve e alle Gaalenghe (AINEVA) c/o Centro sperimento nivometeorologico Via Milano 16A 23032 Bormio
Norway	Norges Geotekniske Institut (Ngl) Postboks 40 Tasen Oslo 8
Switzerland	Eidgenossisches Institut für Schee- und Lawinenforschung (SLF) 7260 Weissfluhjoch Davos
USA	Cold Regions Research and Engineering Laboratory (CRREL) 72 Lyme Road Hanover, NH 03755

It is of vital importance for all those taking part in winter sports to carry an electronic search system and an avalanche shovel, and to be trained in using them. These are the only means that allow a rapid location of accident victims; however, they are not a protection against avalanche accidents.

Comparison with other natural hazards

Compared with earthquakes, tropical storms and floods worldwide, it is obvious that avalanche disasters are neither as spectacular nor as conducive to loss of life and goods. Skiers often view avalanches as harmless and insignificant. But they are frequent events that can be deadly for individuals or groups in every snow-covered mountainous area. And these landscapes are those which tourists find most attractive.

An important difference between avalanches and other natural hazards is that wherever there is snow cover on a steep slope, there is a latent danger of touristic avalanche accident. Therefore, precautions must be taken at almost any time. A hazardous slope can be located beside a safe slope and the avalanche danger can increase within a short time (especially in spring when temperatures are rising during the day).

Moreover, it is more common for the location of an endangered area to coincide with one tourism activity than for other natural hazards. Snow-capped mountains attract active and passive tourists throughout the year but especially in winter. Winter sports enthusiasts are searching for more-or-less untouched steep slopes of deep snow and often pay no attention to avalanche danger.

On the other hand, with an adequate monitoring and warning system, valley avalanches are not as difficult to forecast as, for example, earthquakes, so people can be better prepared.

Conclusion

Mountain climbers and hikers are geographically isolated from any safety service. The lack of familiarity with danger in mountainous areas may limit the perception of risk. Tourists are attracted by landscapes of a larger scale than they are used to. Consequently, they are dependent on broadcast weather and avalanche danger information to avoid being surprised by rapid changes in weather conditions. A simple mountain walk or climb can quickly change into a serious expedition. Foreign tourists in particular may not be used to local climatic characteristics and the mountain environment is naturally hostile, especially in winter. Accidents can happen quickly. In the case of an accident or an evacuation, the harsh winter weather has to be taken into account.

Lack of familiarity with the local language must be taken into account when planning how tourists should be informed in emergencies and in warning sportspeople of touristic avalanches. Most tourists visit a ski area for a short time, without speaking the local language and without knowing where to get information about weather and avalanche danger. That is why those responsible must be active in the distribution of important information in different languages.

CHAPTER VI

EMERGENCY PREPARATIONS AND
POST-DISASTER RELAUNCHING

Introduction

Tourists and tourism destinations are economically, culturally and industrially diverse. Some of the things that are common to them all, however, are day-to-day expectations of a safe, predictable and supportive tourism industry. The resorts and recreation sites that draw tourism depend on both human resources and technology. These two sets of assets must survive not only the routine wear and tear of normal operations, but also the calamities of natural disasters.

Other chapters have discussed the features of natural disasters and the means to build for survival. This chapter presents information on what to do before, during and after a disaster to ensure that resort operations are maintained or are brought back into service as quickly as possible. In a highly competitive market, the local tourism sector can remain competitive under even the most extreme conditions. Managing the event and public perceptions of it is the key to remaining competitive and relaunching the local tourism industry.

In the case of predictable disasters such as tropical storms in the Caribbean or flooding on the Indian subcontinent, there are routine procedures that can be taken to protect both the infrastructure and the market share of local tourism. The resort that disregards routine preparations, annual training and regular updating of emergency procedure manuals places its viability at grave risk. Lengthy and detailed manuals and guidebooks are available on how to plan for emergencies. Listed in the reference section of this chapter, they focus on coordination with local and regional governments, which often have detailed prepared plans on dealing with disasters. The suggestions and tools provided in this chapter draw on experience with earthquakes in Greece and Japan, tropical storms in Mauritius and China, floods in Wales and the United States and emergency action in Sweden, Israel and Argentina.

Regardless of where a resort is be located, when disaster strikes, people must act. If proper planning and training have not been done, steps can still be taken to minimize damage and ensure the protection of the resort, its clients and its staff. Likewise, the local tourism industry that has not developed a marketing strategy for use in the wake of a disaster can still apply sound marketing principles to assist relaunching their tourism. This chapter provides the bare outlines of what to do when confronted with an impending disaster or an unexpected one. The first section provides guidance on emergency precautions resorts and businesses can take. Useful tools for disasters are provided in Appendices A, B and C. The second section deals with recovery and relaunching tourism immediately after the disaster subsides. Marketing and press relations tools are provided in Appendices D and E.

Preparations for a Disaster
Physical Plant Preparations

Regardless of how well designed and built the physical plant of a resort or business, the destructive power of tropical storms, floods and earthquakes cannot be overestimated. This is especially true for those elements of the resort that were never intended to be exposed to such physical abuse — elements such as outdoor leisure equipment, ornaments and decorations, and electronic equipment. Modelled on the approach used in Trou d'Eau Douce, Mauritius, Appendices A, B and C provide checklists that can be used to ensure attention is given to buildings, grounds and equipment before tropical storms and floods.

Key personnel with responsibility for various activities and equipment at a resort should be notified as soon as possible that they will be needed to secure the physical plant. The staff can then refamiliarize itself with emergency procedures and steps necessary to prepare or secure equipment, buildings and important records. They can ensure that emergency equipment and supplies are on hand.

Employee coordination and family preparations

The most important resource of a resort or business is its employees. Because they have homes just as likely to be affected as the resorts and businesses, and have families that are at the top of their priority list, industry managers must give attention to providing guidance and assistance to the staff, especially those who will be needed during the impending disaster. Appendices A, B and C include emergency planning checklists for employee families. These can be copied and should be distributed as early as possible.

Resort management will also want to assess which staff it will need and ensure they are aware of that need. These "critical employees" should be given the opportunity to deal with preparations for their families, and if shelters will be needed, management should examine whether they can assist their employees' families, if in no other manner than through providing transport to government shelters.

Protecting and assisting guests and visitors

Guests in residence expect resort managers to know the local risks and look to them for guidance on what to do when a disaster is imminent or has recently occurred. Appendices A, B and C also offer checklists that resort managers can provide to their guests. A generic version of forms used around the world, they offer practical instruction to guests confronted by storms, floods and earthquakes. Resort managers are encouraged to include the earthquake checklist for tourists among other routine materials as part of in-room information packs. The checklists for tropical storms and floods should be copied and distributed whenever it becomes clear that some form of event is likely to occur.

Disaster relief programs in Israel and England have provided hard won lessons on steps that can be taken to assist local authorities seeking information on the welfare of foreign or out-of-town visitors. (Wyllie, 1994; Ben Hador, 1994) Resorts and hotels should pay special attention to maintaining a list of guests and, when possible, their travel departure plans. When a predictable disaster is expected to arise, tourism managers should be able to inform local government authorities who is in residence, who has departed and where those visitors intended to go. These records are particularly valuable for foreign nationals whose families will attempt to make contact. And this information is of critical value when resorts need to project their preparedness and stability to the tourism market seeking to be reassured.

Guests expected to arrive during or immediately after a predicted disaster are extremely important to the resort. They will gauge the professionalism of the resort by whether they have been given good advice and early warning. The local tourism industry, the local government, and the corporate owners of large resorts and recreational businesses can provide easy assistance to expected guests through a telephone hotline or free call-in telephone number, as discussed below. The resort itself has an additional responsibility to be prepared for questions from guests expected to arrive during or after the onset of a disaster. Information on the status of the hotel and transport facilities should be written and used by the reservations staff and those who handle incoming telephone calls to the hotel or resort. As described in the section on relaunching tourism, these should be updated as appropriate and should be honest yet positive.

Travel Assistance and Transport Coordination

Tourism destinations are dependent on the travel and transport infrastructure. Local and regional governments are responsible for maintaining transport facilities and providing information on the status of roads, bridges, rail and airport facilities. The status of commercial airlines, buses and trains, however, falls to those businesses themselves. Tourist will look to resort managers for information on the status of these services. The resorts and hotels that can provide valuable information on transportation, or other travel assistance, will send a strong message to guests that they are safe, cared for and respected. Everyone involved will recognize that disasters mean that normal operations will be compromised. Resort managers who can keep their guests informed and provide assistance whenever possible will find the guests expressing confidence in the resort and the travel destination.

Communications

Disasters always increase concerns among the families of the travelling public. Further, internal communications within the resort and the resort community can be devastated as well. This lack of communication can be the single greatest source of upset among guests and managers alike. Resort managers can take precautions before the onset of predictable disasters by coordinating with local governments. Knowing how emergency communications will be handled will allow the resort to integrate its own activities with those of others in an effective manner. Large resorts may even have sophisticated communications equipment that will be needed by local government officials.

Internal resort communications should be as sophisticated as the resort itself. Large facilities may need to invest in battery-operated devices that communicate to a central unit at the resort. Small facilities may only need a system where staff check in with a centralized manager on a routine basis. In cases where electronic communications devices are in limited supply, they should first go to critical employees dealing with emergencies or critical engineering and safety equipment.

A major communications need is to keep guests and employees up to date. Facilities with in-house television or speaker announcing systems should use these to make routine updates on the status of the disaster and the resort's response. When power is lost, however, simple bulletin boards, such as those used in large resorts in Mauritius, are extremely effective in keeping guests and staff informed (Morris, 1994). These simple devices can provide information on the storm, the status of tour group plans, travel and evacuation conditions and how to contact friends or family at the resort or in distant homes.

When all else breaks down, resort managers should be prepared with messengers, who can move between buildings, or to government centres, with information on medical emergencies, fires, utility outages and related immediate needs.

Emergency shelter coordination

Large resorts can be expected to serve as emergency shelters when disasters of immense proportion arise. Those buildings made to withstand calamities are more than cost-effective investments by the resort owners. They serve as resources to local governments who may not have municipal resources of equal quality. Experiences in Belarus and Taiwan (Province of China) indicate that when conditions are particularly severe, resorts, hotels and tourism facilities such as museums and exhibition halls may be pressed into service (Gerasimenko, 1994; Ting-Kuei and Fang-Bin, 1994). Managers should be prepared to assist local governments in these crises.

Even when conditions are not severe enough to require evacuation or shelter, resort managers may wish to designate areas within their buildings that are lower in risk. These would include interior rooms for tropical storms, rooms above flood level and structurally sound accommodation after earthquakes.

Shelter management requires significant logistical planning. Food, sanitary facilities, blankets and space must be identified and prepared. Appendices A and B provide checklist sections based on experience from Australia, the United States and Canada that can help organize these preparations, (Heath, 1994; Moore, 1994; MacFarlane, 1994).

Any resort or hotel that will not be able to offer shelter should inform guests where shelter can be found. This information should be broadly distributed and posted prominently. Guests should be apprised of when local governments order evacuations and should be given assistance to comply. Similar assistance should be provided to employee families. Checklist sections on evacuations are provided in Appendices A, B and C, and are based on experience gained in England, China and Argentina, (Norris, 1994; Yuanpeng, 1994).

Security

Disasters can lead to a breakdown in civil law and order. They can also expose the grounds of a resort to the depredations of criminals causing a serious liability risk. Resort managers have viewed security as a service to their guests and employees. In essence, it is a police function that may have to be carried out by the resort. The Canadian emergency site management system provides for direct police participation in disaster management and is a model approach that resorts may wish to use (MacFarlane, 1994). Facilities with limited staff will want to remain in close communication with police and fire departments, as these government units will provide relief from criminals as well as chemical spills and fires. Larger facilities may have the resources to mount their own security efforts. These should still be coordinated with the police, and should be placed on alert before expected disasters.

Resort managers should be prepared to cordon off dangerous sections of their grounds or buildings and blockade access to sections that will not be used, but would provide an opportunity for mischief.

Coordination among industry members to support marketing objectives. Tourism is a competitive business and marketing any particular destination is an ongoing responsibility often shared by the local and state tourism industry. Experience from Greece, Turkey and Israel indicates that a strong marketing effort and appropriate advertising will be important in relaunching the tourism industry in an affected area. (Bar-On and Paz-Tal, 1994). Whenever possible, preparations for these kinds of efforts should be in place before a predictable disaster arises. Even in the event of an unpredicted calamity, the largest and most sophisticated resorts, their parent corporations, and the local and state governments should have some basic preparations available for immediate use. The basic goal is to ensure the long-term confidence of the travelling public in the local industry. If this can be maintained, then tourism in the area will be able to maintain its competitiveness with similar destinations. The key, in addition to a sound marketing strategy, is good press relations.

While marketing tourism destinations is a well-understood activity, the essence of this responsibility changes in the face of a disaster and its aftermath. A lengthy and detailed approach to marketing after disasters is presented in a guidebook by Sonmez *et al* (1994). This guide contains key elements that can be used by resorts, the local industry and the regional or state tourism ministry. It provides a detailed approach that would be most effective in highly developed nations. The five principal concepts, however, are useful everywhere.

As a standing effort, handled well before a disaster arises, the local industry, parent corporations (if any) and tourism ministries should establish an integrated work group to implement these five protective concepts. They should develop a marketing and advertising campaign for print and broadcast media to assist recovery efforts. They should develop advertising strategies appropriate to specific calamities that will signal the start of the relaunching effort. The industry should be prepared to work with the news media and local authorities responsible for press relations. In so doing, they can ensure the marketing message is accurate, effective and properly coupled with other messages being given out by local officials. Fourth, the industry should focus as much positive attention as possible on the destination. Finally, they should inform future visitors of the anticipated recovery period and enhancements expected because of the recovery effort.

These concepts are not done well in the immediate aftermath of a disaster. Resort managers and local tourism industry leaders should take steps to prepare themselves for a relaunching effort before the beginning of the storm or flood seasons, and on a regular basis in areas subject to earthquakes. That said, if nothing has been done, any kind of marketing and media cooperation will pay handsome rewards. The next five sections provide an introduction to the marketing and media-relations challenge facing resort managers and local tourism industry leaders.

Critical pre-disaster marketing actions

Three basic marketing actions are best accomplished no later than during any warning period available before a disaster, and preferably as a routine function before the main tourism season. If local resorts and government ministries have an integrating work group, that body would take on these actions.

First, the local industry should determine what attracts visitors, what makes them want to return and what makes the locale competitive with other destinations. It is also important to know how visitors found out about the destination and what publications they read. This information can be developed through standard market research and may already be available to some of the large resorts or their parent corporations. If this kind of information is not available, interviews with visitors (even immediately before a storm) can provide some of these data.

Second, resort managers, or the industry work group, should maintain a list of advertising outlets for both print and broadcast media that visitors read or view. Contact names, telephone numbers and placement cost information will allow rapid selection of advertising outlets most likely to have a large and positive impact on potential visitors. Research suggests that print media is perceived as more credible than broadcast advertising, and thus should be given emphasis.

Finally, resort managers should launch their advertising campaign as soon as possible and appropriate after the disaster. The news media will direct potential visitors' attention to the destination. Timely advertising that sends a message about the disaster and the locale's resilience will have a higher impact at this time.

Advertising preparations

Advertising is a routine effort within the industry, but is not done overnight. Thus, resorts or industry work groups may want to prepare some materials for use only in the event of a disaster. For example, Caribbean resorts and industry councils have stock advertising copy that needs only minor alterations to become an effective relaunching tool. Resort managers who do not have existing advertising copy may find the following basic rules of assistance:

(a) Have a simple theme, make layouts simple and illustrate the distinctive element of the destination that makes tourists want to visit and to return.

(b) Offer a clear and simple headline which describes the benefits of travelling to the destination.

(c) Use an illustration to attract readers and to tell a story that reinforces the main sales point of the ad.

(d) End the text of an ad with a suggested action a potential visitor may want to take. For example, provide a free telephone number they can call, or a postcard they can mail for information.

(e) Include in the ad the signature of the resort manager (or for very large facilities, a corporate officer) under a promise to serve the visitors honestly and well.

(f) Use a layout that draws the reader to the advertisement, guides the reader through it and presents an overall positive image.

(g) Ensure the text is enthusiastic and sincere, that it emphasizes the positive, minimizes the negative, and is absolutely honest.

(h) Maximize the name of the resort and the location, regardless of the status of recovery from the disaster.

When developing advertising, it is cost-effective to work with other resorts and the state or regional tourism agencies. Ads that link several resorts or nearby destinations also indicate that the visitor will be offered a range of opportunities.

Place ads with those media that previous visitors used to discover your resort and location. Place them in those outlets with the highest degree of public credibility. In order, these are: newspapers, television, magazines and radio. While television can offer a visual effect, print provides memory on paper that can be clipped and saved. This makes it important to include names, addresses and telephone numbers in the text. Take advantage of increased publicity created by the disaster. Increase regular advertising. Thanks to heightened awareness among the public about your destination, advertising done during this period will be more effective and longer lasting.

Immediately after the disaster, plan an "open letter" ad which addresses questions travellers may have about the crisis. This type of ad may have a long body of text, should have a simple visual design to focus attention on content, and works best if signed by a resort manager or local official who would be expected to know what is going on. Advertising placed in the weeks following the "open letter" should begin to relay the message that the crisis situation is reverting back to normal. These ads should emphasize the positive. However, never misrepresent the status of the area or your resort.

Before sending advertising copy to the chosen media outlet, recheck it for interest, clarity, purpose, honesty and credibility. Remember that, because of the nature of the subject, crisis advertising requires additional considerations of integrity and persuasiveness to achieve the desired effect.

A free telephone call-in service

Experiences at tourist destinations in the Middle East and the Mediterranean document the success of information centres that can be accessed by future visitors and families of current visitors (Bar-On and Paz-Tal, 1994). Establishing a toll-free information line is one of the most efficient ways to address concerns expressed by constituents, communicate the status of the crisis situation and gauge public interest. It is important to be prepared to deal with queries by training those who will be answering calls. A sample service line questionnaire is included in Appendix D. Resort managers can add questions relevant to their individual situations to get the utmost use out of information which can be collected over the telephone. Asking questions of callers will help develop greater understanding about the public's concerns and help to determine advertising effectiveness while providing important facts to constituents.

The main purposes of a free call-in service are to answer the public's questions about the disaster; to help control rumours; to offer ways to promote tourism despite the disaster; to record advertising response; and to show concern for those affected by the disaster. Call-in service can be arranged for on a contingency basis during non-crisis times and activated upon the onset of a disaster. Typically, service lines can be activated within 24 hours. Information service lines need not be operated locally. Resorts that are part of international corporations can have corporate partners establish service lines in the nations in which most visitors live.

If a resort or industry work group decides to establish its own local information service line, attention should be paid to the following critical requirements for staff who operate the service:

(a) Staff should be fully informed of the crisis situation. Daily and sometimes hourly updates may be needed.

(b) They should be familiar with the particular telephone system being used, and should be trained before the storm or flood season begins, or as routine training in earthquake-prone areas.

(c) Incoming calls should be answered as quickly, efficiently and politely as possible. Those who want to linger on the line must be told that others are also trying to call in.

(d) Staff should determine if returning calls is appropriate (especially for press queries) and ensure such calls are made rapidly by the most suitable individual.

(e) They should keep a log of all incoming calls, using a report form, if possible (Appendix D).

(f) They should be honest about the situation, but emphasize the positive.

Press Relations

News media representatives gather at the site of impending disasters and quickly arrive after unexpected events. Studies on the role of the media (Sonmez *et al*, 1994) and direct experiences with the media (Hayes, 1994; Kreizelman, 1994) provide a series of suggestions on how best to deal with them.

Reporters are full time investigators with little expertise on any subject related to tourism or disasters. Their purpose is to produce interesting stories about the disaster. The majority are general reporters; only a minority are travel-trade reporters. Resort managers and tourism ministry officials have a year-round duty to maintain relations with the news media. Once notice of an impending disaster arises, or the sudden disaster occurs, the news media will arrive in force. If there is a warning period before a calamity strikes, it pays to establish working relations with the media that can be used once the disaster occurs and the industry is busy trying to deal with emergencies. Media relations fall into two categories — the basic relationship and news conferences.

The media will want to speak to anyone who can help them. All members of the industry should be open to contact, but resort managers should establish a single person from the resort to serve as the spokesperson. A single spokesperson for the local tourism industry may also be desirable as this frees others to deal with problems arising out of the disaster and permits the development of a single basic message for the media in line with the marketing message of hope and recovery. Such a spokesperson should be an individual with experience of meeting the media. He or she should have access to information and have the trust of the local tourism industry. Once appointed, the spokesperson should be the recipient of any information the industry members believe will be sought by the news media.

Resort managers and tourism officials should be proactive. They should contact news media representatives in advance of an impending disaster and should quickly establish a relationship of trust and openness. News conferences, press releases and interviews all aid this effort.

News reporters also have a few requirements. They want honest answers to their questions. Although they will ask about every sensitive issue, they do not really expect you to answer every question or lay bare every distressing event. They will, however, quickly discover any attempt to cover up basic facts. They operate on the clock and need help meeting deadlines. They want information and will respect people who are restrained, professional and open, but will bully anyone if they believe it will get them more information.

They are not experts and want help interpreting the meaning of technical issues and the local and national implications of a disaster. Because they are human and will react to suffering just as much as anyone, they will use and often seek stories of human interest and are not insensitive to reporting on hopes for recovery and renewal. They want representative events and stories about actual people.

Resort managers and those selected to be the media contact should be prepared. Have facts and examples at the ready. Anticipate what reporters will ask, what they want to know and what they are most likely to get wrong if left to their own devices. Be prepared to feed them information so that they won't get facts wrong. Correct them as soon as possible if they make a mistake, and be very polite while doing so. Admit the limits to your knowledge and don't hesitate to ask them what they know.

Be accurate, consistent and on time for press conferences and interviews. If you are responsible for media relations, schedule regular meetings with news media at a location that is easy to get to. Make initial statements and regular updates at these meetings. Offer industry representatives and their resorts for interviews and follow-up, but maintain a stable working relationship with the entire pool of news media representatives through the press conference and news release tools.

Maintain credibility at all times by being honest with the news media. Be organized and professional whether the news is good or bad. Test possible responses and statements for accuracy and timeliness. Keep on top of the story and ahead of the press, at least in regard to your resort and operations. If you are behind, offer to provide corroboration, but do not waste their time. Stay in touch with the media as long as they stay on the story of the disaster.

Deal with rumours by labelling them as such. Regular meetings with the news media will reduce the number of rumours. Particularly destructive rumours deserve to be dealt with through a special press conference and news releases.

Remain available to the press whenever possible and fill any news vacuum that might arise with your message of hope and relaunching. Do not be bashful about this. The press is not bashful. If reporters want access to facts or places, do not hamper them. If it is possible to put forward the industry message, be accommodating. If a particular visit is intended to deal with bad news that has already been given out, be polite, but it is not necessary to offer further assistance. Simply explain that the story is old news and the hope and aspirations of the people living under the gloom of the disaster are the focus of the industry's attention now.

News conferences

As the English example demonstrates, a disaster brings large numbers of reporters into a small area (Hayes, 1994). Often they will be staying at the same lodgings and eating together, especially if hotel accommodations have been reduced as a result of the disaster. Although they are all looking for their own source of facts and their own stories, there is a basic set of facts they all want. These are provided most efficiently through news conferences and press packs. Sample materials for a press pack are provided in Appendix D.

The news conference is simply an opportunity for the resort manager or an appointed media contact to make a statement and answer questions. There are a few rules that news reporters understand and generally respect. Further, there are typical behaviours that reporters will follow. Here are a few principles that, if followed, can make press conferences efficient and effective.

Initiate a schedule of press conferences and release position statements and news releases in the preparatory period before storms and flooding impact the area. Schedule a press conference as soon as possible and practical after earthquakes. Try to schedule conferences in a manner that allows reporters to get stories written and filed by their deadlines. If you don't know when that is, ask the reporters. Disseminate as much accurate information as possible. Tell them what you don't yet know and when you think your information will improve. Work from notes or a briefing book that contains accurate facts. If you are speaking for other resorts, bring specialists who have facts you don't and be prepared to turn to them for answers.

Don't lose control of the press conference. Be in charge of who asks questions, who answers them, when you start and when you end. Maintain a calm and positive manner. Be cooperative and forthright. Journalists want to work quickly. They will ask questions in a manner intended to elicit a response, sometimes giving only two unsatisfactory options for a response. Give them accurate and specific answers to questions and be prepared to reject either option if neither is correct. Give them the correct one or simply say you don't really know, but will attempt to find out. Use the preliminary statement to disseminate most facts and dispel any rumours that have arisen. Acknowledge hearing rumours and give specifics to lay them to rest.

Upon arrival of media members at the site of the press conference, tell them when you will start and be open to informal discussions with them before the start of the conference. Keep such preliminary conversation light and personal. Let them know that basic facts will be given out once the conference begins. Be polite and begin on time. Open the press conference with a self introduction, followed by a prepared statement. Then open the floor to questions. Although many people will attempt to speak at once, acknowledge one person by pointing and saying in a loud, clear voice "Your question please." Allow one follow-up question and then go on to the next person, each time pointing to indicate who is next. Some typical questions and potential answers are provided in Appendix D.

You may chose to prepare packs for the press that contain background information and data on the resort, the damage or the people involved. Distribute these press packs just before the conference begins and have them available after the conference ends. Don't distribute them too early or the reporters are likely to take them and leave.

If other members of the resort management team, or other local resort managers are present, have them wear a name tag and have them sit with the reporters so that they give the impression of being available for further comment after the conference ends. If you don't want them to speak to the press, don't have them at the press conference.

Try to gauge how many people will attend the press conference and hold it in a room that is a little too small, rather than too big, thus avoiding the impression of too little attendance and interest. Invite all members of the media in writing, if possible. Managers of resorts where reporters are staying should be asked to help ensure delivery of invitations. Make the invitations look as official as possible on resort letterhead and signed by the resort manager. Someone should take notes on the press conference to determine what questions were asked, by whom, and what questions were not answered or were answered in a manner that was in any way unsatisfactory. Use this list to prepare for future news releases and conferences. Make sure the reporter asking these questions gets an answer as soon as possible. If television media are present, and especially for interviews, dress in a fashion appropriate to the fact that a disaster has just taken place.

Do not go "off the record" or "on deep background." This implies there are things to be found out that you don't want known. If difficult questions are presented, answer them when appropriate and be honest. If the questions deal with confidential, sensitive or personal matters, tell them that and tell them it would be inappropriate to answer that question at this time. if you feel they have asked a question simply to harass you, tell them you feel as though the question is out of place and won't entertain it. Go on to the next reporter in a professional manner.

Press conferences are working meetings. Food and drink are not appropriate. Breakfast or luncheon meetings should be reserved for public relations efforts and targeted at those reporters who can most assist the relaunching effort. This would include travel-trade writers.

In the wake of a disaster
Once the disaster has struck, resort managers have three major and immediate responsibilities. First and foremost is ensuring the safety of guests, employees and other members of the community. Second is management of the physical recovery from the disaster. Third, and of critical importance, is management of the travelling public's perceptions as a result of the disaster.

Searches and inspections
Emergency operations throughout the world begin with searches for injured persons, dangerous conditions and immediate risks (Feinberg, 1994). Appendices A, B and C provide checklist sections that resort operators can use to organize these searches.

In some cases, especially earthquakes, initial investigations should be done in teams with set deadlines by which they should return. These teams can get into trouble, especially when examining damaged interior spaces, or in the event of secondary explosions and fires. Thus, resort managers should take special precautions to ensure inspections and searches are well organized and to protect the inspectors.

Facility assessments
The first question that guests and employees will want to know is whether damage requires closing the resort. Appendix E provides a tool for making assessments and reporting them to tourism and government ministries, local officials and telephone call-in services.

Security and safety measures

The economic viability of a resort that survives a disaster can be just as easily threatened by liability from preventable accidents in the wake of the disaster. Resort management must get staff to cordon off dangerous areas. This can easily mean closing buildings until utilities are shut down, fires are extinguished, structural damage is assessed and competent engineers indicate the facility is safe for short- or long-term occupancy. Never put guests or employees at risk.

Insurance activities

Before the disaster, valuable materials and papers should have been secured. Once emergency actions have been taken, contact with insurance agents is appropriate. It is useful to record all damage by photo or video, when possible. Records of all repair costs should also be kept.

Guest assistance

As is documented in Israeli reports, special care for tourists at the time of the disaster is essential (Ben-Hador, 1994). If any of the preparations suggested in the previous section have not been taken, they must be accomplished now. Rosters of guests, their health status, travel plans and departure dates must be prepared. Interpreters and local guides should be provided when needed. Contact with local authorities seeking information on foreign or out-of-the area guests will be necessary. Travel assistance for guests will be required, as will be regularly updated information on shelter assistance, health facilities and long-distance telephone access. Once again, the communications bulletin board approach used in Mauritius may become the most useful means for keeping guests and staff informed (Morris, 1994).

The marketing message and press relations

Once the disaster has occurred, the news media will become even more active. This is the time when rumours run rampant and misinformation is easily spread. This is the critical point for ensuring the tourism message gets through. Resorts and the tourism industry are part of a larger community. Tourism has its own voice and its own message that the news media and the travelling public listens to. During and immediately after a crisis, this voice can send a powerful message that will help speed the recovery and relaunching of tourism in the area.

The basic industry message is: what happened, what's going on, and when will things get back to normal. The tourism message always ends with the firm statement that there is a future and travellers will want to be part of it. The message, however, is more than simply the information provided. It is the way that information is given. In particular, the message must convey that the industry is being honest, forthright and sincere.

In general, publicly acknowledge the truth, no matter how negative it is. Deliver bad news fully and first to avoid giving the impression that the resort or the industry is not being honest and open. Learn what the actual status of events is and when you don't know, announce that the range and scope of the problem is being investigated. Then be sure you do investigate them.

Relay relevant facts to the news media and in an "open letter" advertisement, including:

(a) What happened, where and when;
(b) Who was involved;
(c) Who is in charge of crisis management and who is the contact for tourists now in the area;
(d) Who is the contact for travellers who had planned to come to the area in the next few weeks or months;
(e) The most recent developments;
(f) What will be the next steps, what is planned;
(g) The short-term and long-term ramifications for the victims, the community, the general public, the travelling public, the resort and the local tourism industry;
(h) The estimated recovery period; and
(i) What can be confirmed at present about the disaster, what is not known, what is being checked on; when more information will be available; and whom to contact for further information.

Whenever possible, discuss what is being done to correct the situation. Emphasize the positive, such as how many people were saved, the efforts of volunteers and teamwork. Show concern. Cite the resort's participation with regard to politically sensitive issues such as assistance to the impoverished, environmentally sensitive areas, endangered species, and known issues that have brought attention to the area in the recent past.

Convey recovery efforts of the resort, the tourism industry and the community at large. Reassure the news media and the travelling public that the area has responded immediately to the crisis and give examples. When possible, discuss plans for reconstruction, community relief efforts and information on clean-up and basic restoration. Focus on recent positive developments in and around the resort. Place attention on the future.

If mistakes have been made at the resort or within the tourism industry, acknowledge them, apologize immediately and fully. Take responsibility for them and explain what will be done to rectify the problems.

Address issues regarding the extent of damage to the destination and what it will mean to travellers. Put this information in terms of when various recovery events will happen, what risks will continue to exist, what the disaster might mean in terms of costs to the traveller. If the cost of visiting the area is to be reduced because some amenities will not be available, explain this and focus on the economic benefit to the traveller. In every case, demonstrate discretion and promote hope.

APPENDIX A

GUIDE FOR RESORT MANAGERS

WHAT TO DO IN THE EVENT OF A HURRICANE, TYPHOON OR TORNADO

Emergency Preparations

In the event of a tropical storm warning, resort managers will have between a few hours to a couple of days to prepare for the onset of a major storm. This checksheet is designed to remind managers of the key elements they should address to prepare for a storm. It is not intended to replace detailed checklists developed by managers for their own facility. In some cases it may cover equipment not found at a particular resort. It serves merely as a model for use by management to develop their own site-specific checklists. In large facilities, managers may wish to create a separate and highly detailed checklist for each major element of this model, thus allowing staff to take all appropriate precautions, regardless of previous experience or training.

Activating the management team

Identify a person who will take on each of the following eight major responsibilities:

Physical plant _____

Emergency shelter coordination
and supplies _____

Communications _____

Employee coordination _____

Guest roster maintenance _____

Evacuation coordination _____

Travel assistance and
transport coordination _____

Security coordination _____

Physical plant preparations

Verify the status of:

Emergency communications equipment, including radios and mobile telephones

Fire protection systems

Lightning protection systems

Water-level monitoring systems

Overflow detection devices

Automatic shutoffs

Emergency power generation systems

Fuel supplies (top up if possible)

Hazardous materials storage

Define shutdown conditions
Determine who can order shutdown of major physical plant elements (including evacuation).

Determine how a partial shutdown would affect other facility operations.

Verify the length of time required for shutdown and restarting.

Specify the conditions that could necessitate a shutdown and provide this information to the decision-maker in conjunction with information on what parts of the facility would be affected and the time needed to shut down and restart.

Determine who would carry out shutdown procedures.

Initiate shutdowns on command.

Preserve vital records
Secure vital records not needed during the emergency. Store computer tapes and disks in insulated and waterproof containers.

Back up computer systems.

Arrange for evacuation of records to back-up facilities.

Secure outside facilities
Move equipment to protected areas.

Move furniture inside buildings.

Remove banners, flags and vulnerable potted plants and artwork.

Relocate livestock and move pets to indoor facilities.

Secure materials to shutters or protect windows (2 cm marine plywood).

Prepare shelter facilities (if appropriate)
Clear and organize large interior rooms for:

guest and employee occupation;

food, fuel and luggage storage;

food distribution;

sanitary needs (including infant changing and feeding); and

communications.

Provide for emergency heat, lighting and cooking.

Emergency shelter coordination and supplies
Determine for whom the facility will be used as an emergency shelter site (i.e. guests, employees, essential operational employees). Base action on the items below on this decision.

If the facility **WILL NOT** be a shelter, identify official shelters and evacuation sites and prepare directions to them.

If the facility **WILL** provide shelter, verify the accessibility and adequate provision of fuel, food, water, blankets, pillows and first aid supplies to the sheltered areas of the facility. Verify telephone and backup communication lines to civil authorities and emergency assistance.

Communications

Move communications equipment to the shelter space and test it to verify it works. This should include radios and, where possible, telephones and televisions. Battery operated radios and telephones should be included wherever possible.

Distribute portable short-range two-way radios to managers, coordinators, critical facility locations and security staff.

Establish back-up communications procedures which might include human messengers (runners).

Coordinate with civil authorities regarding facility intentions and status.

Establish a Message Board for posting announcements on the status of the storm, warnings, evacuation notices, travel advisories and telephone numbers for assistance and emergencies.

Copy and distribute checksheets and advisory notices for tourists and guests.

Employee coordination

Identify and notify critical employees needed at the facility for preparation or maintenance and operation during the storm.

Provide checksheets and advisory notices to employees and their families.

Determine the need for employee sheltering and inform shelter coordinators.

Guest and employee roster

Provide a log for guest and employee sign-in and sign-out.

Prepare and maintain a roster of current employees and guests.

Establish a file in which to maintain data provided by guests about their home addresses, emergency family contacts and travel plans.

Upon evacuation, update the roster with information on departures and intended destinations.

Evacuation coordination

Determine evacuation conditions for the various categories of tourists, guests, non-critical employees and critical employees.

Verify who makes the decision to evacuate the facility.

Determine and post the evacuation routes and destination points.

Establish notification procedures to announce an evacuation.

Upon the decision to evacuate, contact civil authorities on facility intentions and evacuation progress.

Travel assistance

Identify commercial and emergency travel coordinators for airline, train and bus lines.

Announce the availability of emergency travel assistance.

Contact tour directors and determine transport requirements and the availability of any additional seats, if they have their own transport. Post the availability of such opportunities.

Security coordination

Determine security requirements during emergency preparations, onset of the storm and immediately after the storm.

Establish when security resources should be brought to the facility and when they should be deployed.

Identify a coordination centre for security resources and supply it with appropriate emergency communications equipment.

Coordinate with communications in the event of security problems and the need for civil assistance.

What to do during a hurricane, typhoon or tornado

Personal safety

Regardless of any other responsibilities, all resort employees (especially managers) should take adequate steps for their own personal safety. The people who count on you need you alive and well when the storm abates. Be sure to:

Stay indoors and away from windows. Go to the designated shelter area. Do not be fooled if there is a lull, it could be the eye of a hurricane.
Leave a parked vehicle, trailer or temporary structure immediately and go to the resort shelter.

If in a car as the force of the storm begins to build, drive to the nearest shelter. Stay near your resort as the storm warning period expires. Once the storm force begins, do not drive.

Listen to the radio or television for information.

Whenever possible, exhibit a calm confident manner. Advise patience and safety.

Shelter supervision

As the storm warning period expires and the force of the storm begins to show, move all guests and personnel into sheltered areas of the resort.

Turn on radios and television so that everyone knows what is going on. Conserve battery-operated equipment for use when electrical service is interrupted.

Establish an area for people who want quiet space in which to rest. If the space is available, give those who wish it a room in which to meditate or pray.

Provide board games, cards and puzzles to children and parents.

Clearly label and staff a table or desk at which sheltered occupants can seek information or assistance.

Maintain a shelter roster and log-in/log-out books at exits. Advise strongly against anyone leaving the sheltered areas of the resort during the storm, especially during a calm likely to be associated with the eye of the storm.

Maintain the information bulletin board.

What to do immediately after a hurricane
Upon cessation of the storm, advise guests and non-critical employees to remain in the shelter for a few minutes until the safety of the grounds can be assessed and dangerous conditions can be identified and marked.

Conduct a search of the facility premises (outdoor and indoors) looking for:

Injured people;

Downed electrical and telephone lines;

Broken gas, water or sewage lines;

Damaged structures, missing windows, walls, roofs, ceilings, or buildings that have moved off their foundations;

Fires, spilled hazardous substances, trapped gases or volatile substances, and other immediate dangers.

Once security staff have assessed the resort grounds and reported dangerous areas, announce areas, buildings and rooms to avoid and ask the employees and guests to take the following precautions:

Stay away from areas marked by security as closed or off-limits as there are dangerous conditions there.

Look out for broken glass and downed power lines.

Report injured people to the shelter assistance desk or other appropriate contact point (front desk). Do not attempt to move seriously injured persons unless they are in immediate danger of death or further injury.

Stay away from damaged areas in the community unless authorities ask for your help.

Drive only when necessary until streets have been cleared and civil authorities announce the integrity of bridges and causeways.

Stay away from beaches, river banks and streams until potential flooding and storm surf have subsided.

Use great caution when entering damaged buildings and rooms. Be sure that walls, ceilings and roof are in place and that structures rest firmly on their foundations. Beware of snakes and vermin that may have been dislodged by the storm.

Inform authorities of power, water or sewage line outages.

Post where to get emergency medical assistance at the resort or elsewhere within the community.

Convert space, as necessary, to offer medical assistance.

Record all damage (video cameras can be very useful in this regard).

Determine the status of electrical and fuel supplies and whether restart of equipment can be accomplished safely. Restart only critical equipment so as not to overload potentially compromised electrical supplies.

Verify the safety of restarts, especially when utility lines may service damaged buildings and thus create fire and explosion potential.

Assess facility capacities and the need for relocation of some or all guests. If relocation is necessary, initiate contact with civil authorities and alternative resort managers who may be able to accept guests. Be prepared to advise incoming guests of facility conditions. (See the section on relaunching tourism after a disaster.)

Routinely post notices of important information, especially on the status of your facility and other important venues (e.g. restaurants, telephone service, electrical service and transport).

Maintain your guest roster and be prepared to notify authorities of the status and location of your guests.

Inform employees of the resort status, how the resort can help their families and when they should return to work or go home.

WHAT TO DO IN THE EVENT OF A FLOOD

Emergency Preparations

In the event of a flood, resort managers will have between a few hours and a couple of days to prepare for the onset of flooding. This checksheet is designed to remind managers of the key elements they should address to pre-pare for high water. It is not intended to replace detailed checklists developed by managers for their own resort. In some cases it may cover equipment not found at a particular resort. It serves merely as a model for use by manage-ment to develop their own site-specific checklists. In large facilities, managers may wish to create a separate and highly detailed checklist for each major element of this model, thus allowing staff to take all appropriate precautions, regardless of previous experience or training.

Activating the Management Team

Identify a person who will take on each of the following eight major responsi-bilities:

Physical plant _____

Emergency shelter coordination and supplies _____

Communications _____

Employee coordination _____

Guest roster maintenance _____

Evacuation coordination _____

Travel assistance and transport coordination_____

Security coordination _____

Physical plant preparations

Verify the status of:

Emergency communications equipment including radios and mobile tele-phones

Fire protection systems

Lightning protection systems

Water-level monitoring systems

Overflow detection devices

Automatic shutoffs

Emergency power generation systems

Hazardous materials storage

Define shutdown conditions:

Determine who can order shutdown of major physical plant elements (includ-ing evacuation).

Determine how a partial shutdown would affect other facility operations.

Verify the length of time required for shutdown and restarting.

Specify the conditions that could necessitate a shutdown and provide this information to the decision maker. Also supply information on what parts of the facility would be affected and the time needed to shut down and restart.

Determine who would carry out shutdown procedures.

Initiate shutdowns on command.

Preserve vital records
Secure vital records not needed during the emergency.

Back up computer systems.

Arrange for evacuation of records to backup facilities.

Store computer tapes and disks in insulated and waterproof containers.

Secure outside facilities
Move equipment to protected areas.

Move furniture inside buildings.

Remove banners, flags and vulnerable potted plants and artwork.

Relocate livestock and pets to indoor facilities.

Floodproofing measures
Acquire portable water pumps, generators and fuel.

Acquire plastic liners, sand and bags.

Line vulnerable exterior walls with the plastic sheeting, secured by a sandbag wall.

Prepare shelter facilities(if appropriate)
Clear and organize large interior rooms for:

guest and employee occupation;

food, fuel and luggage storage;

food distribution;

sanitary needs (including infant changing and feeding); and

communications.

Provide for emergency heat, lighting and cooking.

Preventive clean water flooding of basements
If flooding of subground floors is inevitable, permit the floodwaters to flow freely into the basement of buildings (or flood the basement yourself with clean water, if you are sure it will be flooded anyway). This will avoid structural damage to the foundations and the building by equalising the pressure on the outside of the basement walls and floors.

Emergency shelter coordination and supplies

Determine for whom the facility will be used as an emergency shelter site (i.e. guests, employees, essential operational employees). Base action on the items below on this decision.

If the facility WILL NOT be a shelter, identify official shelters and evacuation sites and prepare directions to them.

If the facility WILL provide shelter, verify the accessibility and adequate provision of fuel, food, water, blankets, pillows and first-aid supplies to the sheltered areas of the facility.

Verify telephone and back-up communication lines to civil authorities and emergency assistance. If access to safe drinking water is likely to be compromised, fill available storage tanks, including bathtubs and boilers. Ensure they are cleaned before filling.

Communications

Move communications equipment to the shelter space and test it to verify it works. This should include radios, and where possible, telephones and televisions. Battery-operated radios and telephones (if available) should be included wherever possible.

Distribute portable short-range two-way radios to managers, coordinators, critical facility locations and security staff.

Establish backup communications procedures which might include human messengers (runners).

Coordinate with civil authorities regarding facility intentions and status.

Establish a Message Board for posting announcements on the status of the flood, warnings, evacuation notices, travel advisories, and telephone numbers for assistance and emergencies.

Copy and distribute checksheets and advisory notices for tourists and guests.

Employee coordination

Identify and notify critical employees needed at the facility for preparation or maintenance and operation during the flood.

Provide checksheets and advisory notices to employees and their families.

Determine the need for employee sheltering and inform shelter coordinators.

Guest and employee roster

Provide a log for guest and employee sign-in and sign-out.

Prepare and maintain a roster of current employees and guests.

Establish a file in which to maintain data provided by guests about their home addresses, emergency family contacts, and travel plans.

If an evacuation is required, update the roster with information on departures and intended destinations.

Evacuation coordination

Determine evacuation conditions for the various categories of tourists, guests, non-critical employees and critical employees.

Verify who makes the decision to evacuate the facility.

Determine and post the evacuation routes and destination points.

Establish notification procedures to announce an evacuation.

Upon the decision to evacuate, contact civil authorities on facility intentions and evacuation progress.

Travel assistance

Identify commercial and emergency travel coordinators for airline, train and bus lines.

Announce the availability of emergency travel assistance.

Contact tour directors and determine transport requirements and the availability of any additional seats, if they have their own transport. Post the availability of such opportunities.

Security coordination

Determine security requirements during emergency preparations, onset of the flood and immediately after the flood.

Establish when security resources should be brought to the facility and when they should be deployed.

Identify a coordination centre for security resources and supply it with appropriate emergency communication equipment.

Coordinate with communications in the event of security problems and the need for civil assistance.

What to do during a flood

Personal safety

Regardless of any other responsibilities, all resort employees (especially managers) should take adequate steps for their own personal safety. The people who count on you need you alive and well when the flood abates. Be sure to:

Listen to the radio or television for information.

Whenever possible, exhibit a calm confident manner. Advise patience and safety.

Stay away from beaches, river banks and streams until potential flooding and storm surf have subsided.

Use great caution when entering damaged buildings and rooms. Be sure that walls, ceilings and roof are in place and that structures rest firmly on their foundations. Beware of snakes and vermin that may have been dislodged by the floodwaters.

Drive carefully, as the integrity of streets, bridges and causeways may have been compromised by floodwaters and flood conditions. Do not drive into flooded areas. If floodwaters rise around your car, abandon the car and move to higher ground immediately, if you can do so safely. You and your vehicle can be quickly swept away as flood waters rise.

Be aware of flash flood potential. If there is any possibility of a flash flood occurring, move immediately to higher ground. Do not wait for instructions to move. Do not walk through moving water. Fifteen centimeters of moving water can knock you off your feet. If you must walk in a flooded area, walk where the water is not moving. Use a stick to check the firmness of the ground in front of you.

Stay away from flood waters. They may be contaminated by oil, petrol or raw sewage. The water may also be electrically charged from underground or downed power lines.

Instruct all employees and guests to be careful of health and safety practices. Everyone should wash their hands with soap and clean water whenever they come in contact with flood waters. Drink only water known to be safe. Listen for reports from the authorities on the safety of tap water. Boil water for three minutes if the safety of it can not be determined.

Shelter supervision

When flood conditions lead civil authorities to order evacuation, evacuate all guests and personnel. Turn on radios and television so that everyone knows what is going on. Conserve battery-operated equipment for use when electrical service is interrupted.

Establish an area for people who want quiet space in which to rest. If the space is available, give those who wish it a room in which to meditate or pray.

Provide board games, cards and puzzles to children and parents.

Clearly label and staff a table or desk at which sheltered occupants can seek information or assistance.

Maintain a shelter roster and log-in/log-out books at exits.

Maintain an information bulletin board.

Look out for flood-strewn waste and downed power lines.

Report injured people to emergency medical facilities or other appropriate contact points. Do not attempt to move seriously injured persons unless they are in immediate danger of death or further injury.

Convert space, as necessary, to support medical assistance.

What to do after a flood

If your resort has sustained damage, contact your insurance agent. If your policy covers your situation, prepare for the agent's visit:

Take photos or videotape of post-flood resort conditions.

Separate damaged and undamaged materials and assets.

Locate your insurance and financial records.

Keep detailed records of clean-up costs.

WHAT TO DO IN THE EVENT OF AN EARTHQUAKE

Personal safety
Regardless of any other responsibilities, all resort personnel (especially managers) should take adequate steps for their own personal safety. The people
who count on you need you alive and well after the initial quake. Be sure to
do the following:

If you are indoors, take cover under a sturdy desk, table or bench, or against
an inside wall, and hold on. Stay away from glass, windows, outside doors or
walls and anything that could fall, such as lighting fixtures or furniture.

If you are outdoors, stay there. Move away from buildings, street lights and
utility wires.

In a crowded public place, do not rush for a doorway — other people will have
the same idea. Take cover, and move away from display shelves containing
objects that can fall.

In a high-rise building, get under a sturdy desk, away from windows and outside walls. Stay in the building on the same floor, an evacuation may not be
necessary. Be aware that the electricity may go out or the sprinkler systems
or fire alarms may go on. Do not use elevators.

In a moving vehicle, stop as quickly as safety permits and stay in the vehicle.
Avoid stopping near or under buildings, on overpasses, or near trees or utility
wires. After the earth stops shaking, proceed cautiously, watching for road
and bridge damage.

Whenever possible, exhibit a calm, confident manner. Advise patience and safety.

After the earthquake
Be prepared for aftershocks. These are usually less violent than the main quake
but can be strong enough to do additional damage to weakened structures.

Assemble the resort's management team at an outside location in the resort. If
you have no pre-arranged meeting location, once outside, identify an easily
recognisable landmark and tell staff to meet there immediately. Ask them to
spread the word. If there is no pre-designated emergency management team, or
if key management staff are missing, select key staff to help on the tasks below.

Inspections
Assign someone to check outside the buildings for injured people. Do not
attempt to move seriously injured persons unless they are in immediate danger of death or further injury. If you must move an unconscious person, first
stabilize the neck and back, then call for help immediately.

Assign inspection teams of no fewer than two people and begin facility damage inspection from the outside of buildings only. Visually inspect utility lines
and appliances for damage. Have an initial report made at a set time no
longer than half an hour after the teams begin initial inspections. If, after one-
half hour an inspection team fails to report (in person or by radio), stop further inspections and begin a search.

If outside inspections suggest it is safe to enter buildings, and the senior resort manager approves it, assign teams to check inside the resort for structural damage. If you have doubts about safety, have buildings inspected by a professional before entering. Warn inspectors on the following:

If the electricity goes out, use flashlights or battery powered lanterns. DO NOT USE CANDLES, MATCHES OR OPEN FLAMES indoors after the earthquake because of possible gas leaks.

If gas is smelled or a hissing or blowing sound heard, open a window and leave the building immediately.

Do not use elevators until fully tested.

Stay away from windows, skylights and items that could fall.

Inspect interior space for non-structural damage. Open cabinets cautiously. Beware of objects that can fall off shelves.

Have an initial report made at a set time no longer than half an hour after the team begins its initial inspection. If, after one-half hour an inspection team fails to report, begin a search. Call out for the inspector, rather than enter a damaged building or room. Allow no one else into those areas of the resort until civil authorities or other experts are on the scene.

Utility cut-off
In the event of an apparent gas leak, shut off the main outside gas valve. Report the leak to the gas utility from a neighbouring location. Stay out of the building. If the gas supply is shut off at the main valve, do not turn it back on without the approval of the gas utility or until an inspection confirming that all appliances are set for start-up.

If there is electrical damage, switch off all electrical power at the main fuse box or circuit breaker.

If water pipes are damaged, shut off the water supply at the main valve.

Do not flush toilets until you know that sewage lines are intact.

If your resort has sustained damage:
Assess the need for evacuation and relocation of guests. Contact local authorities for locations of shelters and alternative lodging.

Contact your insurance agent. If your policy covers your situation, prepare for the agent's visit:

Take photos or videotape of post-earthquake resort conditions.

Separate damaged and undamaged materials and assets.

Locate your insurance and financial records.

Keep detailed records of clean-up costs.

Initial Recovery Response

Interior building clean-up

Rope off all dangerous areas such as spilled hazardous materials, entries to damaged buildings, and all elevators not yet status tested.

Clean up spilled medicines, bleaches, gasoline and other flammable liquids inside buildings. Evacuate the building if gasoline or other chemical fumes are heavy and the building is not well ventilated.

If water is cut off, use water from the water heater or other known clean sources. Minimize water use if future supplies of clean water are expected to be small. If the quality of drinking water is uncertain, boil it for three minutes before drinking.

Have chimneys inspected for damage before lighting a fire.

Communications

Construct a message board for use by management, guests and staff to alert them to new information, evacuation orders, or any other information they might need to deal with the emergency.

Distribute to staff and guests copies of the earthquake checksheets designed for them.

Post the checksheets and highlight the following instructions:

If possible, stay off the streets. If people must go out, they should be warned to watch for hazards created by the earthquake, such as fallen objects, downed electrical wires, weakened walls, bridges, roads and sidewalks.

Stay away from damaged areas, unless assistance has been specifically requested by police, fire or relief organisations.

If near coastal waters, be aware of possible tsunamis (tidal waves). When local authorities issue a tsunami warning, assume that a series of dangerous waves is on the way. Stay away from the beach and evacuate beachfront property until local authorities say it is safe to return.

Guest and employee roster

Prepare and maintain a roster of current employees and guests.

Establish a file in which to maintain data provided by guests about their home addresses, emergency family contacts and travel plans.

Provide a log for guest and employee sign-in and sign-out.

If the resort must be evacuated, update the roster with information on departures and intended destinations.

Evacuation coordination

Determine evacuation conditions for the various categories of tourists, guests, non-critical employees and critical employees.

Verify who makes the decision to evacuate the resort or any of its buildings.

Determine and post the evacuation routes and destination points to shelters or alternative resorts.

Establish notification procedures to announce an evacuation.

Upon the decision to evacuate, contact civil authorities on facility intentions and evacuation progress.

Travel assistance
Identify commercial and emergency travel coordinators for airline, train and bus lines.

Announce the availability of emergency travel assistance within the resort, or the lack thereof.

Contact tour directors and determine transport requirements and the availability of any additional seats, if they have their own transport. Post the availability of such opportunities.

Security coordination
Establish when security resources should be brought to the resort and when they should be deployed.

Identify a coordination centre for security resources and supply it with appropriate emergency communication equipment.

Coordinate with communications in the event of security problems and the need for civil assistance.

APPENDIX B

GUIDE FOR TOURISTS

WHAT TO DO IN THE EVENT OF A TROPICAL STORM, HURRICANE OR TORNADO

What to do during a tropical storm, hurricane or typhoon
Stay indoors and away from windows. Go to the basement, storm cellar or designated shelter area. If there is no basement, go to an interior room on the lower level (interior hallways). Do not be fooled if there is a lull in the storm, it could be the eye of a hurricane.

Leave a parked vehicle, trailer or mobile home immediately and go to a more substantial structure.

If in a car as the force of the storm begins to build, drive to the nearest substantial structure and seek shelter there.

Listen to the radio or television for information.

Avoid using the telephone except for serious emergencies. Local authorities need first priority on telephone lines.

What to do during a tornado
Be alert for approaching storms. When a tornado has been sighted, go to your shelter immediately. Stay away from windows, doors and outside walls.

In a house or small building, go to the basement or storm cellar. If there is no basement, go to an interior room on the lower level (cupboards, interior hallways). Get under a sturdy table, hold on and protect your head. Stay there until the danger has passed.

In a school, nursing home, hospital, factory or shopping centre, go to predesignated shelter areas. Interior hallways on the lowest floor are usually safest. Stay away from windows and open spaces.

In a high-rise building, go to a small, interior room or hallway on the lowest floor possible.

Leave a vehicle, trailer or mobile home immediately, and go to a more substantial structure.

If there is no shelter nearby, lie flat in the nearest ditch, ravine or culvert with your hands shielding your head.

Leave a car and take shelter in a nearby building. Do not attempt to out-drive a tornado. They are erratic and move swiftly.

What to do immediately after a hurricane or tornado
If you are in a safe location, stay where you are until local authorities say it is safe to leave. If you have evacuated the community, do not return until authorities say it is safe to return.

When the storm has fully subsided, report your condition and location to the resort management.

Look for the Resort Message Board and keep tuned to local radio or television stations for information about where to find medical help, and how to find temporary shelter or travel assistance.

Look our for broken glass and downed power lines. Check for injuries. Do not attempt to move seriously injured persons unless they are in immediate danger of death or further injury.

Stay away from damaged areas unless local authorities request volunteers. If you are needed, bring your own drinking water, food and sleeping gear.

Drive only when necessary. The streets will be filled with debris. Roads may be blocked or weakened.

Stay away from beach fronts, river banks and streams until potential flooding has passed. Stay away from downed power lines and report them to the power company. Report broken gas, sewer or water mains.

Use great caution when entering a damaged building. Be sure that walls, ceiling and roof are in place and that the structure rests firmly on the foundation. Do not enter without the permission of the owners. Beware of snakes and vermin that may have been dislodged by the storm.

Emergency preparations checklist
If a storm warning is given, meet with travel party members and tour directors to discuss the dangers of severe weather and under what conditions your trip should be curtailed. Review the sections on how to respond if a tropical storm is imminent.

Contact your tour director or hotel staff for information on evacuation warning systems and travel coordinators in case of the need for evacuation.

Determine how a tour manager will notify you if a tour is to be curtailed. If you are travelling on your own, decide which conditions must arise for you to shorten your trip and return home. Recognize that you are not the only person or group making these decisions, and seek assistance from travel coordinators at the resort or transport venues.

Identify the location of the resort's emergency notification bulletin boards, and if necessary, the emergency shelters designated by your hotel management.

Prepare a list of your travel party and their family contacts and telephone numbers. Provide this to the resort management and keep a copy with you.

Each time you leave the resort, keep staff informed of where you are going and who is in your travel party. Leave this information on a note in a prominent place in your room as well.

Be attentive to radio and television weather updates and instructions from authorities.

Pick one distant and one local friend, relative, tour director or resort manager for family members to call if separated during a storm. (It can be easier to call long distance than within the affected area.)

Keep family records and travel papers in a waterproof container. Include airline tickets, insurance policies, family identification and health care records.

Pack clothes and other items not in use and be prepared to finish packing quickly, if an evacuation of the area is imminent.

If you are told to evacuate the area

Listen to a radio for the location of emergency shelters and other evacuation information. Follow instructions of local officials.

Check the resort's emergency notification board for information on where your travel party should gather for meetings, travel planning, relocation or transport to airports, trains or buses.

Wear sensible clothing and sturdy shoes and use travel routes specified by local officials.

Let the hotel know when you left and where you are going. Leave a note to that effect in your room and with the front desk.

Do not delay your evacuation.

WHAT TO DO IN THE EVENT OF SEVERE RAIN STORMS AND FLOODING

What to do during heavy rains

Be aware of the potential for flash floods. If there is any possibility of a flash flood occurring, move immediately to higher ground. Do not wait for instructions to move.

Listen to radio or television stations for local information.

Stay away from flood waters. They could be contaminated. Do not walk through moving water. Fifteen centimetres of moving water can knock you off your feet. If you must walk in a flooded area, walk where the water is not moving. Use a stick to check the firmness of the ground in front of you.

Do not drive into flooded areas. If floodwaters rise around your car, abandon the car and move to higher ground as long as you can do so safely. You and your vehicle can be quickly swept away as floodwaters rise.

What to do during a flood

When the rain has stopped, report your condition and location to the resort management.

Stay away from floodwaters. They may be contaminated by oil, gasoline or raw sewage. The water may also be electrically charged from underground or downed power lines.

Use common sense health and safety practices. Anyone who comes into contact with floodwaters should wash their hands with soap and clean water. Drink only water known to be safe. Listen for reports from the authorities on the safety of tap water.

Stay away from moving water deeper than 15 centimetres. If you must walk through water, walk only in areas where it is calm and unmoving. Stay away from downed power lines and report them to the power company.

Be aware of areas where flood waters may have receded. Roads and bridges may have weakened and could collapse under weight of a car.

Stay away from disaster areas unless authorities ask for volunteers.

Keep tuned to local radio or television stations for information about where to find medical help, and how to find temporary shelter or travel assistance.

Emergency preparations checklist

If a flood warning is given, meet with travel party members and tour directors to discuss the dangers of severe weather and under what conditions your trip should be curtailed. Review the sections on how to respond if a tropical storm is imminent.

Contact your tour director or hotel staff for information on evacuation warning systems and travel coordinators in case of the need for evacuation.

Determine how a tour manager will notify you if a tour is to be curtailed. If you are travelling on your own, decide what conditions must arise for you to shorten your trip and return home. Recognize that you are not the only person or group making these decisions, and seek assistance from travel coordinators at the resort or transport venues.

Identify the location of the resort's emergency notification bulletin boards, and if necessary, the emergency shelters designated by your hotel management.

Prepare a list of your travel party and their family contacts and telephone numbers. Provide this to the resort management and keep a copy with you.

Each time you leave the resort, keep staff informed of where you are going and who is in your travel party. Leave this information on a note in a prominent place in your room as well.

Be attentive to radio and television weather updates and instructions from authorities.

Pick one distant and one local friend, relative, tour director or resort manager for family members to call if separated during a storm. (It can be easier to call long distance than within the affected area.)

Keep family records and travel papers in a waterproof container. Include airline tickets, insurance policies, family identification and health care records.

Pack clothes and other items not in use and be prepared to finish packing quickly, if an evacuation of the area is imminent.

If you are told to evacuate the area

Listen to a radio for the location of emergency shelters and other evacuation information. Follow instructions of local officials.

Check the resort's emergency notification board for information on where your travel party should gather for meetings, travel planning, relocation or transport to airports, trains or buses.

Wear sensible clothing and sturdy shoes and use travel routes specified by local officials.

Let the hotel know when you left and where you are going. Leave a note to that effect in your room and with the front desk.

Do not delay your evacuation.

WHAT TO DO IN THE EVENT OF AN EARTHQUAKE

What to do during an earthquake

If you are indoors, take cover under a sturdy desk, table or bench, or against an inside wall, and hold on. Stay away from glass, windows, outside doors or walls and anything that could fall, such as lighting fixtures or furniture.

If you are outdoors, stay there. Move away from buildings, street lights and utility wires.

In a crowded public place, do not rush for a doorway — other people will have the same idea. Take cover, and move away from display shelves containing objects that can fall.

In a high-rise building, get under a sturdy desk, away from windows and outside walls. Stay in the building on the same floor, an evacuation may not be necessary. Be aware that the electricity may go out or the sprinkler system or fire alarm may be activated. Do not use elevators.

In a moving vehicle, stop as quickly as safety permits, and stay in the vehicle. Avoid stopping near or under buildings, on overpasses, or near trees or utility wires. Then proceed cautiously, watching for road and bridge damage.

What to do after an earthquake

When the earthquake has fully subsided, report your condition and location to the resort management and your tour director.

Be prepared for aftershocks, These are usually less violent than the main quake but can be strong enough to do additional damage to weakened structure.

Check for injuries. Do not attempt to move seriously injured persons unless they are in immediate danger of death or further injury. Evacuate any building where you can smell natural gas, or when gasoline or other chemical fumes are heavy and the building is not well ventilated.

If you smell gas or hear a hissing or blowing sound, open a window and leave the building. If it is your responsibility, shut off the main gas valve outside if you can. Report the leak to the gas company from some other location. Stay out of the building.

If there is electrical damage, notify the property manager. If it is your responsibility, switch off all electrical power at the main fuse box or circuit breaker.

If water pipes are damaged, shut off the water supply at the main valve.

Do not flush toilets until you know that sewage lines are intact.

If water is cut off, drink only that water you know is safe. Water boiled for three minutes is usually safe, as are recognized brands of properly sealed bottled water.

Open cabinets cautiously. Beware of objects that can fall off shelves.

Use the telephone only to report a life-threatening emergency.

Listen to news reports for the latest emergency information. Check emergency notification bulletin boards at your resort for:

Information on the need to go to shelters or curtail your travel;

The status of transport systems and how to get travel assistance;

Where your travel group should check in; and

How to contact officials to let them and your family know of your condition.

Stay off the streets. If you must go out, watch for hazards created by the earthquake, such as fallen objects, downed electrical wires, weakened walls, bridges, roads and pavements.

Stay away from damaged areas unless your assistance has been specifically requested by police, fire or relief organisations.

If you are near coastal waters, be aware of possible tsunamis, also known as tidal waves. When local authorities issue a tsunami warning, assume that a series of dangerous waves is on the way. Stay away from the beach and evacuate beach front property until local authorities say it is safe to return.

APPENDIX C

FAMILY GUIDE

WHAT TO DO IN THE EVENT OF A TROPICAL STORM, HURRICANE OR TORNADO

If there is a hurricane or tornado warning
Listen for information and instructions on radio or television newscasts. Verify your location in relation to areas reported to be at risk. Learn when decisions will be made on the need for evacuations from your area.

Contact household members. Make sure everyone knows where to meet and whom to call in case you are separated. Consider the needs of relatives and others with special needs.

Gather several days supply of water and food for each family member. Clean and fill the bathtub to ensure a supply of clean water. Assemble or check an emergency supplies kit (using the checklist below).

Secure materials that could be thrown around by the wind. Place small objects inside buildings. Overturn tables and benches to reduce wind resistance and tie them together and to well-secured objects such as trees. Secure shutters on windows.

Prepare to evacuate. Fuel your car. Review evacuation routes and planned meeting places. If instructed, turn off utilities at the main valves.

Evacuate to a safe location IF:
Authorities announce an evacuation and you live in an evacuation zone;
You live in a mobile home/caravan or temporary structure;
You are threatened by a hurricane and live on the coast, on a floodplain near a river or inland waterway; or
You feel you are in danger.

When authorities order an evacuation:

Leave immediately to avoid being marooned by flooded roads or fallen trees.

Follow evacuation routes announced by local officials.

Stay away from coastal areas, river banks and streams until potential flooding is past. .

Tell others where you are going.

During a hurricane
Stay indoors and away from windows. Go to the basement, storm cellar or designated shelter area. If there is no basement, go to an interior room on the lower level (interior hallways). Do not be fooled if there is a lull in the storm, it could be the eye of a hurricane.

Leave a parked vehicle, trailer or caravan immediately and go to a more substantial structure.

If in a car as the force of the storm begins to build, drive to the nearest substantial structure and seek shelter.

Listen to the radio or television for information.

Avoid using the telephone except for serious emergencies. Local authorities need first priority.

During a tornado

When a tornado has been sighted, go to a shelter immediately. Stay away from windows, doors and outside walls.

In a house or small building, to the basement or storm cellar. If there is no basement, go to an interior room on the lower level (closets, interior hallways). Get under a sturdy table, hold on and protect your head. Stay there until the danger has passed.

In a school, nursing home, hospital, factory or shopping centre, go to pre-designated shelter areas. Interior hallways on the lowest floor are usually safest.

Stay away from windows and open spaces.

In a high-rise building, go to a small, interior room or hallway on the lowest floor possible.

Leave a vehicle, trailer or caravan immediately and go to a more substantial structure.

If there is no shelter nearby, lie flat in the nearest ditch, ravine or culvert with your hands shielding your head.

In a car, get out and take shelter in a nearby building. Do not attempt to outdrive a tornado. They are erratic.

What to do immediately after a hurricane or tornado

Stay where you are if you are in a safe location until local authorities say it is safe to leave. If you evacuated the community, do not return until authorities say it is safe to return.

Keep tuned to local radio or television stations for information about caring for your family, where to find medical help, and how to find temporary shelter or assistance.

Look out for broken glass and downed power lines.

Check for injuries. Do not attempt to move seriously injured persons unless they are in immediate danger of death or further injury.

Stay away from disaster areas unless local authorities request volunteers. If you are needed, bring your own drinking water, food and sleeping gear.

Drive only when necessary. The streets will be filled with debris. Roads may be blocked or have weakened.

Stay away from river banks and streams until potential flooding has passed. Stay away from downed power lines and report them to the power company. Report broken gas, sewer or water mains.

Use great caution when entering a damaged building. Be sure that walls, ceiling and roof are in place and that the structure rests firmly on the foundation. Wear sturdy work boots and gloves. Beware of snakes and vermin that may have been dislodged by the storm.

Create an emergency plan
Complete this checklist on an annual basis, perhaps on a special family day such as a birthday or anniversary. If there is early warning of a possible natural disaster, do as many of these as possible:

Meet household members to discuss the dangers of fire, severe weather, earthquakes and other emergencies. Look at the rest of this guide and explain how to respond.

Find the safe spots in your home for protection in case of a violent storm.

Discuss what to do about power outages and personal injuries.

Walk through your home. Identify the escape routes from each room and show family members how to turn off the water, gas and electricity at main switches when necessary.

Post emergency telephone numbers near telephones.

Emergency preparations
Teach children how and when to call for fire and police assistance.

Instruct household members to turn on the radio for emergency information.

Pick one distant and one local friend or relative for family members to call if separated during a disaster. (It is often easier to call long-distance than within the affected area.)

Pick two emergency meeting places: (1) a place near your home in case of a fire; and, (2) a place outside your neighbourhood in case you cannot return home after a disaster.

Keep family records in a waterproof and fireproof container. Include insurance policies, family identification and health care records.

Discuss what to do with family pets or livestock.

If you need to evacuate
Listen to a radio for the location of emergency shelters. Follow instructions of local officials.

Wear protective clothing and sturdy shoes.

Take your Disaster Supplies Kit.

Lock your house.

Use travel routes specified by local officials.

If you are sure you have time, shut off water, gas and electricity if instructed to do so.

Let others know when you left and where you are going.

Make arrangements for pets. Animals may not be allowed in public shelters.

Prepare a disaster supplies kit

Assemble supplies you might need in an evacuation. Store them in an easy-to-carry container such as a backpack or duffel bag. If a car will be used for the evacuation, ensure additional car-related supplies are stored in the vehicle.

Include: a supply of water (2 litres per person per day). Store water in sealed, unbreakable containers. Use only fresh, safe water.

A supply of non-perishable packaged or canned food and a manual can opener.

A change of clothing, rain gear and sturdy shoes for each person in the family. Even children can carry their own.

Blankets or sleeping bags.

A first aid kit and prescription medications (including extra glasses).

A battery-powered radio, flashlights and extra batteries.

Cash and credit cards.

An extra set of car keys.

A list of important family information, including a list of family physicians; out-of-town family contacts; special medical conditions; and the style and serial number of medical devices such as pacemakers.

Special items for infants, elderly or disabled family members.

For car evacuations include booster cables, fire extinguishers (all purpose), tire repair kit and pump, maps, a shovel and flares.

WHAT TO DO IN THE EVENT OF A FLOOD

What to do when there is an immediate flood threat

Determine if you are in a flood-prone area. Identify dams and levees in your area and whether you are at risk if they fall.

Listen for information and instructions on radio or television newscasts. Learn when decisions will be made on the need for evacuations from your area.

Contact household members. Make sure everyone knows where to meet and whom to call in case you are separated. Consider the needs of relatives and others with special needs.

Assemble or check an emergency supplies kit (using the checklist below). Clean and fill the bathtub to ensure a supply of clean water.

If you have time, move valuable furniture, electronics equipment, rugs and important papers to upper floors, or transport them to the homes of family members or friends whose property will not be flooded. Bring outdoor garden equipment and lawn furniture inside or tie it down.

Prepare to evacuate. Fuel your car. Review evacuation routes and planned meeting places. If instructed, turn off utilities at the main valves.

Evacuate to a safe location IF:
Authorities announce an evacuation and you live in an evacuation zone;
You live in a mobile home/caravan or temporary structure;
You live on a flood-plain near a river or inland waterway; or
You feel you are in danger.
When authorities order an evacuation:
Leave immediately to avoid being marooned by flooded roads or fallen trees.

Follow evacuation routes announced by local officials.

Stay away from coastal areas, river banks and streams until potential flooding is past.

Tell others where you are going.

What to do during heavy rains

Be aware of flash floods. If there is any possibility of a flash flood occurring, move immediately to higher ground. Do not wait for instructions to move.

Listen to radio or television stations for local information.

Do not walk through moving water. Fifteen centimeters of moving water can knock you off your feet. If you must walk in a flooded area, walk where the water is not moving. Use a stick to check the firmness of the ground in front of you.

Do not drive into flooded areas. If flood waters rise around your car, abandon the car and move to higher ground, if you can do so safely. You and your vehicle can be quickly swept away as flood waters rise.

When deep flooding is likely, permit the flood waters to flow freely into the basement of your home, (or flood the basement yourself with clean water, if you are sure it will be flooded anyway). This will avoid structural damage to the foundations and the house by equalising the water pressure on the outside of the basement walls and floors.

What to do after a flood

Stay away from flood waters.They may be contaminated by oil, gasoline or raw sewage. The water may also be electrically charged from underground or downed power lines.

Instruct all family members to be careful of health and safety practices. Everyone should wash their hands with soap and clean water whenever they have come into contact with flood waters. Drink only water known to be safe. Listen for reports from the authorities on the safety of tap water. Boil water for three minutes if the safety of it can not be determined.

Stay away from moving water deeper than 15 centimetres.

Stay away from downed power lines and report them to the power company.

Be aware of areas where flood waters may have receded. Roads and bridges may have weakened and could collapse under the weight of a car.

Stay away from disaster areas unless authorities ask for volunteers.

Keep tuned to local radio or television stations for information about caring for your family, where to find medical help and how to find temporary shelter or assistance.

If your house has sustained damage, contact your insurance agent. If your policy covers your situation, prepare for the agent's visit:

(a)   Take photos or videotape of your belongings and your home.
(b)   Separate damaged and undamaged belongings.
(c)   Locate your insurance and financial records.
(d)   Keep detailed records of clean-up costs.

If you need to evacuate

Listen to a radio for the location of emergency shelters. Follow instructions of local officials.

Wear protective clothing and sturdy shoes.

Take your Disaster Supplies Kit.

Lock your home.

Use travel routes specified by local officials.

Let others know when you left and where you are going.

If you are sure you have time, shut off water, gas and electricity if instructed to do so.

Make arrangements for pets. Animals may not be allowed in public shelters.

A Disaster Supplies Kit

Assemble supplies you might need in an evacuation. Store them in an easy-to-carry container such as a backpack or duffel bag. If a car will be used for an evacuation, ensure additional car-related supplies are stored in the vehicle.

Include: A supply of water (2 litres per person per day). Store water in sealed, unbreakable containers. Use only fresh, safe water.

A supply of non-perishable packaged or canned food and a manual can opener.

A change of clothing, rain gear and sturdy shoes for each person in the family. Even children can carry their own.

Blankets or sleeping bags.

A first aid kit and prescription medications (including extra glasses).

A battery-powered radio, flashlights and extra batteries.

Cash and credit cards.

An extra set of car keys.

A list of important family information, including: a list of family physicians; out-of-town family contacts; special medical conditions; and the style and serial number of medical devices such as pacemakers.

Special items for infants, elderly or disabled family members.

For car evacuations include booster cables; fire extinguishers (all purpose), tire repair kit and pump, maps, a shovel and flares.

WHAT TO DO IN THE EVENT OF AN EARTHQUAKE

What to do during an earthquake

If you are indoors, take cover under a sturdy desk, table or bench, or against an inside wall, and hold on. Stay away from glass, windows, outside doors or walls and anything that could fall, such as lighting fixtures or furniture.

If you are outdoors, stay there. Move away from buildings, street lights and utility wires.

In a crowded public place, do not rush for a doorway — other people will have the same idea. Take cover, and move away from display shelves containing objects that can fall.

In a high-rise building, get under a sturdy desk, away from windows and outside walls. Stay in the building on the same floor, an evacuation may not be necessary. Be aware that the electricity may go out or the sprinkler systems or fire alarms may go on. Do not use elevators.

In a moving vehicle, stop as quickly as safety permits and stay in the vehicle. Avoid stopping near or under buildings, on overpasses, or near trees or utility wires. Then proceed cautiously, watching for road and bridge damage.

After the earthquake

Be prepared for aftershocks. These are usually less violent than the main quake but can be strong enough to do additional damage to weakened structures.

Check for injured people. Do not attempt to move seriously injured persons unless they are in immediate danger of death or further injury. If you must move an unconscious person, first stabilize the neck and back, then call for help immediately.

If the electricity goes out, use flashlights or battery powered lanterns. DO NOT USE CANDLES, MATCHES OR OPEN FLAMES indoors after the earthquake because of possible gas leaks.

Check your home for structural damage. If you have doubts about safety, have the home inspected by a professional before entering. Have your chimneys inspected for damage before lighting a fire.

Clean up spilled medicines, bleaches, gasoline and other flammable liquids inside buildings. Evacuate the building if gasoline or other chemical fumes are heavy and the building is not well ventilated.

Visually inspect utility lines and appliances for damage.

If you smell gas or hear a hissing or blowing sound, open a window and leave the building. Shut off the main gas valve outside, if you can. Report the leak to the gas company from a neighbour's house. Stay out of the building. If you shut off the gas supply at the main valve, you will need a professional to turn it back on.

If there is electrical damage, switch off all electrical power at the main fuse box or circuit breaker.

If water pipes are damaged, shut off the water supply at the main valve.

Do not flush toilets until you know that sewage lines are intact.

If water is cut off, use water from the water heater or other known clean sources. If the quality of drinking water is uncertain, boil it for three minutes before drinking.

Open cabinets cautiously. Beware of objects that can fall off shelves.

Use the phone only to report a life-threatening emergency.

Stay off the streets. If you must go out, watch for hazards created by the earthquake, such as fallen objects, downed electrical wires, weakened walls, bridges, roads and sidewalks.

Stay away from damaged areas unless your assistance has been specifically requested by police, fire or relief organisations.

If you live near coastal waters, be aware of possible tsunamis, also known as tidal waves. When local authorities issue a tsunami warning, assume that a series of dangerous waves is on the way. Stay away from the beach and evacuate beachfront property until local authorities say it is safe to return.

If you need to evacuate
Listen to a radio for the location of emergency shelters. Follow instructions of local officials.

Wear protective clothing and sturdy shoes and take your Disaster Supplies Kit.

Lock your home.

Use travel routes specified by local officials.

If you are sure you have time, shut off water, gas and electricity, if instructed to do so.

Let others know when you left and where you are going.

Make arrangements for pets. Animals may not be allowed in public shelters.

A Disaster Supplies Kit

Assemble supplies you might need in an evacuation. Store them in an easy-to-carry container such as a backpack or duffel bag. If a car will be used for an evacuation, ensure additional car-related supplies are stored in the vehicle.

Include:

A supply of water (2 litres per person per day). Store water in sealed, unbreakable containers. Use only fresh, safe water.

A supply of non-perishable packaged or canned food and a manual can opener.

A change of clothing, rain gear and sturdy shoes for each person in the family. Even children can carry their own .

Blankets or sleeping bags.

A first aid kit and prescription medication (including extra glasses).

A battery-powered radio, flashlights and extra batteries.

Cash and credit cards.

An extra set of car keys.

A list of important family information, including a list of family physicians; out-of-town family contacts; special medical conditions; and the style and serial number of medical devices such as pacemakers.

Special items for infants, elderly or disabled family members.

For car evacuations include booster cables; fire extinguishers (all purpose), tire repair kit and pump, maps, a shovel and flares.

APPENDIX D

GUIDANCE ON MARKETING AND PRESS RELATIONS ASSOCIATED WITH RELAUNCHING TOURISM AFTER A DISASTER

1.   Sample Questions and Answers

A review of questions asked of resort managers and public officials during and after disasters serves up the following questions and potential answers.

Q.   This (storm, flood, earthquake) has been predicted for many days/months/years. Why wasn't something done to prepare for it?

A.   Prediction of these types of events is always difficult, and (name the officials or their organisations) did provide us with early warning (if they did). As a result, we made a variety of preparations such as (describe some specifics that resulted in lives saved and property protected).

Q.   How can the families of tourists find out if their relatives are safe?

A.   Resorts are developing rosters of their guests and will be coordinating with local authorities. Local officials have established contacts with embassies and missions, and are providing them names of people known to be safe. We are also making every effort to provide telephone lines for our guests to call their homes and reassure their families. (Make sure this is true before you say it.)

Q.   Do you know how many people died at your resort?

A.   Local officials are keeping track of injuries and deaths. We know of only (number) injuries or deaths at (your resort) and will release the names of the people only after we have informed their families. (Press representatives from their home nations/cities may be able to help make notifications, but must be cautioned to hold such information until it is clear families have been properly notified.)

Q.   How long will the resort be closed?

A.   (This should have been addressed in the opening statement.) We are assessing the damage right now. We don't have a prediction yet, but will provide one shortly after we complete our damage assessment. We hope to have one within (xxx hours), and will provide it to you at the next press briefing.

(If this question has been addressed at an earlier session...) We have previously suggested it will take xxx days/months before the resort can be reopened. That estimate remains our best estimate. (Or) We have revised our estimate and now expect the resort to reopen on (name the time and day).

Q.   How much damage was done?

A.   We cannot estimate the damage until all our evaluations are completed. We hope to do that by (name the time and day).

Q.   When will it be safe for tourists to come to the area?

A.   (Specific venues) are open now. (Specific venues) are expected to be back in operation on (give a date certain). Travellers seeking information on specific locations I haven't mentioned should feel free to contact (the free call-in line, the chamber of commerce, an industry contact person) at the following telephone number (give them only one number).

Q.   How will the disaster affect the tourism industry in this area?

A.   In the short term, we have to recover and rebuild. Our local offerings will be limited for a short while (name a date if possible). The area is not uniformly affected, however, and some resorts are already open for business. In time, the effect of this disaster will produce a safer and better travel destination, and by (name a time) we believe tourists will find this area better than it ever was before.

2.   The Press Pack

Press packs are folders containing information useful to the news media and in line with the industry message. These are to be distributed immediately before press conferences. Typical enclosures are copies of the prepared statement of the spokesperson, fact sheets, position statements (if different from prepared statements) and news releases.

The press pack should include an index of contents if there is any significant amount of material. The right hand side of the packet folder should contain news releases, fact sheets, quote sheets from spokespersons, and any position statements that are being made.

The left side of the folder should contain background information such as the history of the area and its tourism attractions, its growth and future plans. Photographs of the disaster and especially of reopened resorts and special attractions should also be included, with complete information on their location and the source of the photographs. The name, address and telephone/fax numbers of the spokesperson should be prominently displayed in the press pack.

News releases can also be distributed in the absence of a full press pack. They should be mailed or hand delivered to all members of the news corps.

The final pages of this appendix contain sample position statements, news releases and fact sheets.

The following principles are useful to those preparing news releases:

Have a brief and accurate headline which presents the most important facts of the story and attracts the reader's attention. The headline should use verbs but should not start with one. The message should have an active voice.

Use short sentences. The first and last paragraphs should be short.

Be positive and include the industry message of hope and relaunching.

Structure the story, placing the most important facts first.

Cover all the facts. Stay away from opinions. Restrict quotations to positive statements from resort management.

Have several people review the statement for accuracy and unintended implications before putting it into final form and distribution.

Provide answers in all written documentation and attachments on the who, what, where, when, why and how of the disaster and specific events arising out of the natural causes.

When possible, and in good taste, provide estimates on the extent of damage, injuries, immediate responses of victims, witnesses and resort managers. Include the human interest elements of the story, giving specifics.

Constantly gather and incorporate new material into news releases. Stay ahead of the news media. Monitor the news and challenge wrong reporting with specific facts.

Release information important to relaunching tourism first, saving more mundane or unimportant information until later or for others.

Include contact persons and telephone numbers in all releases.

Provide news releases to the media throughout the world, targeting those places where your travel clientele most frequently originate.

Develop a directory of press and broadcast contacts, if this was not done during any warning period before a disaster. To do this, consult media directories.

Minimize the bad and maximize the good news.

Type news releases on resort letterhead, or the letterhead of a tourism council, on standard size paper using only one side of the paper and normal business margins.

If information is being given to only one particular outlet, for example a travel reporter in your key clients' home territory, type EXCLUSIVE on it and do not distribute it to any other news outlets.

Indicate on the news release the urgency of the information and any restrictions on its release. Mark, for example, FOR IMMEDIATE RELEASE, RELEASE AT YOUR CONVENIENCE, or FOR RELEASE ON (date)

Identify the specific individual in each news publication who should receive the release and send it only to that person at that publication. If you don't have a specific name, send the release to the editor-in-chief and NOT to the advertising department.

SAMPLE NEWS RELEASE
(Location Specific) Tourism Council
(or) XYZ Resort
Address
Telephone Number
Fax Number

(Contact: Spokesperson) FOR IMMEDIATE RELEASE

Telephone Number

Alternative Contact

Telephone Number

(DISASTER) PROMPTS EMERGENCY ACTION FROM THE (AREA) TOURISM COUNCIL (OR FROM THE XYZ RESORT)

(CITY/STATE) (Month, Day) The XYZ Resort (or Area Tourism Council) has begun crisis management activities as a result of the recent (DISASTER) in (NAME OF DESTINATION), according to (Name), spokesman for the XYZ Resort (or Area Tourism Council).

The (DISASTER), which has affected large areas of the state (area and attractions) coastal area, golf courses and tourism operations, has damaged (number of hectares) of state and private property, (number of) trees and (number of) homes and private buildings. (DESCRIBE IMPACTS OF DISASTER ON AREA, POPULATION AND TRAVEL AND TOURISM INDUSTRY, FOCUSING ON CLOSINGS AND REOPENINGS.) The XYZ Resort (Area Tourism Council) is taking all possible steps to assist the (AREA's) local travel and tourism industry to recover from this setback and prepare for the coming tourism season.

Current activities include (GIVE LOCATION AND RESORT SPECIFIC INFORMATION).

Travellers seeking specific information on resorts and other venues may contact. (GIVE EITHER A FREE CALL-IN HOTLINE NUMBER OR DIRECT THEM TO THE RESORTS AND VENUES.)

(NAME), spokesperson for the (Name the resort or organisation), expresses confidence that some resorts and tourist attractions will be reopened by (GIVE DATE) and encourages people interested in (AREA NAME) to contact their travel agents and the (Free Call-in Hotline or Chamber of Commerce) for updates on the status of the area. In remarks made immediately after the (DISASTER) Mr. Mrs. Ms. (Name) said:

"(USE SOME POSITIVE AND HOPEFUL QUOTE.)"

SAMPLE FACT SHEET FOR TOURIST DESTINATION
(Location Specific) Tourism Council (or) XYZ Resort
Address
Telephone Number
Fax Number

Contact:	(Spokesperson) Telephone Number
Area:	The hub of Southern Xlan's coastal shoreline — a 150-mile stretch of coral reefs and tropical forest preserves — this area accounts for one-fifth of the region's annual tourism revenues.
Population:	About 25 000 permanent residents from North Beach to Southern Point. During the high season, the non-tourist resident populations grow to about 37 000.
Annual Visitors:	Daily pass-through visitors number 50 000, with overnight visitors consisting of an additional 40 000 people. Some 75 per cent of visitors come from the north-west of the nation with the remainder being international travellers.
Economic Impact:	In 1993 tourism accounted for over $1.5 billion, about 55 per cent of Xlan's total revenue from travel and tourism. Development of this area for tourism has grown at a steady rate of around 8 per cent each year since 1985, when the first commercial hotel and beach resort opened its doors.
Accomm.:	More than 400 businesses rent accommodation, providing 42 000 rooms, including hotels, motels, condominiums and cottages.
Restaurants:	More than 650 food service establishments are available, serving all types of cuisine, including seafood and tropical Xlan fare.
Camping:	Three county campgrounds and one national park campground provide facilities for 350 individual sites. About 15 per cent of these will accommodate hookups for caravans.
Recreation:	There are more than 120 charter fishing boats servicing this area. Twenty licensed dive instructors provide tours of the reef, a protected national maritime sanctuary. There are 30 commercial and three state tours of the tropical rain forest, also a protected area. More than 237 protected or endangered species live in these waters and forests.
Golf:	There are 41 golf courses, of which 37 are open to the public. Fees range from $35 to $185.
Last hurricane:	Hurricane Yosemite hit the Xian coast with top winds of 130 miles per hour on 31 August, 1977. While the northern coastal region received mild rain and flooding damage, the majority of this coastal area has not been struck by a major storm in recorded history.

SAMPLE FACT SHEET FOR TOURIST INDUSTRY COUNCIL
(Location Specific) Tourism Council
Address
Telephone Number
Fax Number

CONTACT: Name

Telephone

(Alternative Contact)

Telephone

PURPOSE OF COUNCIL: The Tourism Council is a non-profit organisation committed to assisting the (AREA's NAME) tourism industry recover as quickly and smoothly as possible from disasters which may occur.

ESTABLISHED: (Provide date)

COUNCIL OFFICES: (Provide address)

HOTLINE NUMBER: A Free Call-In telephone number is supported by the Council (give number).

IMMEDIATE RECOVERY   (List major efforts under way.)
EFFORTS:

FUTURE PLANS: (List future development, advertising and public relations efforts planned.)

INDUSTRY   Accommodation, attractions, food and beverage
REPRESENTATION: establishments, and support services.

MEMBERS: (Identify officers, contact persons and major venues and establishments that are key members, e.g. board members and major funding sources.)

SAMPLE POSITION OR PUBLIC STATEMENT OF
THE (TOURISM COUNCIL/RESORT) ON THE (NATURAL DISASTER)
Tourism Council or XYZ Resort
Address
Telephone Number
Fax Number

Contact: Name

Telephone

The XYZ Resort (or Tourism Council) is deeply saddened by the loss of life, health and property resulting from the (DISASTER). We extend our condolences to the victims of the tragedy and stand ready to help our guests, employees, their families, the community and our business community in any and every way possible.

Each of the tourism industry members in the area was making efforts to prepare for this type of disaster long before it actually happened. (MAKE SURE THIS IS TRUE BEFORE YOU SAY IT.) Staff members took part in seminars and training on how to deal with emergencies in the event of a (TYPE OF DISASTER).

As we re-establish communications with resort managers and other tourism organizations in the area, we will share what we learn about the extent of damages and the availability of resources with the public as soon as possible. We know there are concerned citizens and relatives who are anxious about the extent of the damage and we are committed to doing everything we can to disseminate the information we receive.

We also recognize that relatives of our guests may be worried about the health and welfare of their family members in our area. We will take every step possible to assemble information on the status of guests at our resort and coordinate directly with local authorities to provide lists of the visitors we are now serving.

In addition, we are mobilising a relief effort to assist the local tourism industry. Those who wish to participate in that effort, or who want information on the status of the resort and other attractions in the area may contact us at a free call-in number (PROVIDE TELEPHONE AND FAX NUMBERS).

We have begun assessment of the damage and will provide information on facilities that are open and reopening as soon as it becomes available to us. We realize that we have a responsibility to the people of (NAME OF AREA) and the travelling public who vacation here. We have a special environment that we want to preserve for everyone, even when circumstances beyond our control make that responsibility difficult to fulfil. We are committed to having (NAME OF AREA) functioning and available to visitors again as soon as possible. We have every hope that we will be in your plans again very soon.

CALL-IN HOTLINE QUESTIONNAIRE
(To be filled out by Hotline Operators)

Thank you for calling. We appreciate your interest. How can we help you?

1. Identify caller's concerns

    _____

    _____

    _____

2. If they want general information, inform them.

    The status of our situation is:

    The (DISASTER) occurred at: _____

    (Time, place, area affected) _____

    Damage includes:

    Injured_____

    Dead _____

    Cost of damages _____

Facilities that are open include: (Provide list of resorts and attractions that are open.)

Facilities that are not yet open, but expect to reopen within a week are: (Give list.)

Facilities that will be closed for an extended period are: (Give list.)

Would you mind if we ask you a few questions so that we may send you more information about our area upon further recovery? Thank you.

Name _____

Address _____

Phone (if appropriate) _____

Where did you see or hear about our Call-in Hotline?

_____

Do you have a confirmed reservation in the area and will you still be coming?

_____

Thank you for your call.

APPENDIX E

SAMPLE DAMAGE ASSESSMENT REPORT

(To be filled out by resort managers and provided to the Call-in Hotline.)

GENERAL INFORMATION

1. Name of resort _____

2. Address of resort _____

3. Telephone and Fax of resort_____

4. Contact person and title at resort _____

5. Type of service provided by the resort _____

    _____

DAMAGE INFORMATION

6. General description and extent of damage:

    _____

7. Resort is:_____ damaged but still operable_____ damaged, requires minor repairs_____ inoperable but could reopen with major repairs _____destroyed.

8. Resort is accessible by _____

9. Resort is dependent on (gas) (water) (sewerage) (electric) (telephone) utilities and can not reopen until (utility repairs) (emergency utilities) (alternative services) are provided (delete as appropriate).

10. Estimated number of days resort may be out of operation

    _____

11. Estimate of uninsured loss to the facility (damage and lost revenues)

    _____

EMPLOYMENT INFORMATION

12. Total employment provided by the resort _____

13. Estimate of number of days employees may be out of work_____

14. Number of employees who will be entitled to receive unemployment insurance _____

VISITOR PERCEPTIONS/RUMOURS/MEDIA COVERAGE

15. What feelings about the crisis situation and recovery efforts have visitors expressed?

_____

16. What damaging rumours have you or your staff heard? From what source?

_____

17. What negative media coverage have you seen or heard? From what source?

_____

ADDITIONAL COMMENTS

Return this form to:

(Tourism Council Contact Address and Fax)

REFERENCES

CHAPTERS I AND II

Bibliography

Bar-On, Raphael R. and Paz-Tal, Gershon, "Minimising and measuring the effects of disasters on tourism", *Abstracts of the First International Congress on Local Authorities Confronting Disasters and Emergencies,* Union of Local Authorities in Israel, Tel-Aviv, 1994.

Ben Hador, Avi, "Special care for tourists at the time of disaster", *Abstracts of the First International Congress on Local Authorities Confronting Disasters and Emergencies,* Union of Local Authorities in Israel, Tel-Aviv, 1994.

Kreizelman, David, "The emergency press center in Tel Aviv during the Persian Gulf War", *Abstracts of the First International Congress on Local Authorities Confronting Disasters and Emergencies,* Union of Local Authorities in Israel, Tel-Aviv, 1994.

Moore, Avagene, "Trends in emergency management", *Abstracts of the First International Congress on Local Authorities Confronting Disasters and Emergencies,* Union of Local Authorities in Israel, Tel-Aviv, 1994.

Morris, Charles L., "Cyclone drill and staff action", Le Touessrok Hotel, Trou d'Eau Douce, Mauritius. Personal Communication, 17 June 1994.

Sonmez, S.F. Backman, S.J. and Allen, L.A., *Managing Tourism Crises: A Guidebook,* Department of Parks, Recreation and Tourism Management, Clemson University, Clemson, S.C, USA, 1994.

References

ESCAP/WMO/LRCS, *Guidelines for Disaster Prevention and Preparedness,* WMO, Geneva, 1977.

Plate, E., "Risk management and assessment of natural hazards", paper presented at the World Conference on Natural Disaster Reduction, WMO, Geneva, 1994.

Sheets, R.C., "Risk management and assessment of natural hazards", paper presented at the World Conference on Natural Disaster Reduction, WMO, Geneva, 1994.

Smith, D.K., *Natural Disaster Reduction: How Meteorological and Hydrological Services can help,* WMO-No. 722, WMO, Geneva, 1989.

UNDRO, *Mitigating Natural Disasters: Phenomena, Effects and Options.* A Manual for Policy Makers and Planners, UN, New York, 1991.

WMO, *The role of the World Meteorological Organization in the International Decade for Natural Disaster Reduction,* WMO-No. 745, Geneva, 1990.

WMO, *Will there be a tropical cyclone with your name?,* Fact Sheet No. 11, WMO, Geneva, 1993.

Additional sources and further reading

Bar-On, Raphael R. and Paz-Tal, Gershon, "Minimising and measuring the effects of disasters on tourism", *Abstracts of the First International*

Congress on Local Authorities Confronting Disasters and Emergencies,
Union of Local Authorities in Israel, Tel-Aviv, 1994.

Bates, R.J., *Disaster Recovery Planning,* McGraw-Hill, New York, 1992.

Ben Hador, Avi, "Special care for tourists at the time of disaster", *Abstracts of
the First International Congress on Local Authorities Confronting Disasters
and Emergencies,* Union of Local Authorities in Israel, Tel-Aviv, 1994.

Berge, D.T., *The First 24 Hours,* Basil Blackwell, Cambridge, MA, USA, 1992.

Hayes, Peter, "The management of an organization in crisis", *Abstracts of the
First International Congress on Local Authorities Confronting Disasters
and Emergencies,* Union of Local Authorities in Israel, Tel-Aviv, 1994.

Littlejohn, R.F., Crisis Management: *A Team Approach,* American
Management Association, New York, 1983.

MacFarlane, Gordon J., "Emergency site management", *Abstracts of the First
International Congress on Local Authorities Confronting Disasters and
Emergencies,* Union of Local Authorities in Israel, Tel-Aviv, 1994.

Moore, Avagene, "Trends in emergency management", *Abstracts of the First
International Congress on Local Authorities Confronting Disasters and
Emergencies,* Union of Local Authorities in Israel, Tel-Aviv, 1994.

Morris, Charles L., "Cyclone drill and staff action ", Le Touessrok Hotel, Trou
d'Eau Douce, Mauritius. Personal Communication, 17 June, 1994.

Smith, J., *The Publicity Kit,* John Wiley, New York, 1991.

Sonmez, S.F., Backman, S.J. and Allen, L.A., *Managing Tourism Crises: A
Guidebook,* Department of Parks, Recreation and Tourism Management,
Clemson University, Clemson, SC, USA, 1994.

Ting-Kuei, Tsay and Fang-Bin, Lin, "Confronting potential disasters of Taipei
county area in Taiwan", *Abstracts of the First International Congress on
Local Authorities Confronting Disasters and Emergencies,* Union of Local
Authorities in Israel, Tel-Aviv, 1994.

US Federal Emergency Management Agency, *Guide for the Development of
State and Local Emergency Operations Plans,* Publication CPG 1-8,
Washington, DC, September 1990.

US Federal Emergency Management Agency, *Are You Ready?* Publication H-
34, Washington, DC, September 1993.

US Federal Emergency Management Agency, *Home Study Course on The
Emergency Program Manager,* Publication IS-1, Washington, DC,
September 1993.

US Federal Emergency Management Agency, *Emergency Management Guide
for Business & Industry,* Publication FEMA 141, Washington, DC,
October 1993.

Wyllie, Bob, "Volunteers in emergencies in the UK", *Abstracts of the First
International Congress on Local Authorities Confronting Disasters and
Emergencies,* Union of Local Authorities in Israel, Tel-Aviv, 1994.

Yuanpeng, Song, "Shanghai chemical emergency accident preparedness and
rescue programme", *Abstracts of the First International Congress on
Local Authorities Confronting Disasters and Emergencies,* Union of Local
Authorities in Israel, Tel-Aviv, 1994.

CHAPTER III

References

Askew, Arthur J, "Flooding: contributions from the engineering profession and an international perspective", paper presented at Hazards Forum Seminar, Institution of Civil Engineers, London, January 1992.

ESCAP/WMO/LRCS, *Guidelines for Disaster Prevention and Preparedness in Tropical Cyclone Areas,* Geneva/Bangkok, Economic and Social Commission for Asia and the Pacific, World Meteorological Organization and League of Red Cross Societies, 1977.

Handmer, J.W., Guidelines for Floodplain acquisition, *Applied Geography,* 7, 1987, pp. 203-21.

Houghton, J.T., Jenkins, G.J., and Ephraums, J.J. eds, *Climate Change: The IPCC Scientific Assessment,* Cambridge, Cambridge University Press, 1990.

Hoyt, W.G. and Langbein, W.B., *Eastern Waters Study: Strategies to manage flood and drought in the Ganges Brahmaputra basin,* Washington, DC, US Agency for International Development, 1955.

Sheaffer, J.R., *Flood Proofing: An element in a flood damage reduction program,* Chicago, IL, University of Chicago, Department of Geography Research, Paper no 65, 1960.

Smith, Keith, *Environment Hazards: Assessing Risk and Reducing Disaster,* London.

Additional sources

Bar-On, Raphael R. and Paz-Tal, Gershon, "Minimising and measuring the effects of disasters on tourism", *Abstracts of the First International Congress on Local Authorities Confronting Disasters and Emergencies,* Union of Local Authorities in Israel, Tel-Aviv, 1994.

Bates, R.J., *Disaster Recovery Planning,* McGraw-Hill, New York, 1992.

Ben Hador, Avi, "Special care for tourists at the time of disaster", *Abstracts of the First International Congress on Local Authorities Confronting Disasters and Emergencies,* Union of Local Authorities in Israel, Tel-Aviv, 1994.

Berge, D.T., *The First 24 Hours,* Basil Blackwell, Cambridge, MA, USA, 1992.

Hayes, Peter, "The management of an organization in crisis", *Abstracts of the First International Congress on Local Authorities Confronting Disasters and Emergencies,* Union of Local Authorities in Israel, Tel-Aviv, 1994.

Littlejohn, R.F., *Crisis Management: A Team Approach,* American Management Association, New York, 1983.

MacFarlane, Gordon J., "Emergency site management", *Abstracts of the First International Congress on Local Authorities Confronting Disasters and Emergencies,* Union of Local Authorities in Israel, Tel-Aviv, 1994.

Smith, J., *The Publicity Kit,* John Wiley, New York, 1991.

Moore, Avagene, "Trends in emergency management", *Abstracts of the First International Congress on Local Authorities Confronting Disasters and Emergencies,* Union of Local Authorities in Israel, Tel-Aviv, 1994.

Sonmez, S.F., Backman, S.J. and Allen, L.A., *Managing Tourism Crises: A Guidebook,* Department of Parks, Recreation and Tourism Management, Clemson University, Clemson, SC, USA, 1994.

UNDRO, a list of disaster management-related terms with their definitions to be included in an internationally agreed multilingual glossary, Geneva, UNDRO Secretariat, 1991.

US Federal Emergency Management Agency, *Are You Ready?*, Publication H-34, Washington, DC, September 1993.

US Federal Emergency Management Agency, *Guide for the Development of State and Local Emergency Operations Plans,* Publication CPG 1-8, Washington, DC, September 1990.

US Federal Emergency Management Agency, *Home Study Course on The Emergency Program Manager,* Publication IS-1, Washington, DC, September 1993.

US Federal Emergency Management Agency, *Emergency Management Guide for Business & Industry,* Publication FEMA 141, Washington, DC, October 1993.

Wyllie, Bob, "Volunteers in emergencies in the UK", *Abstracts of the First International Congress on Local Authorities Confronting Disasters and Emergencies,* Union of Local Authorities in Israel, Tel-Aviv, 1994.

CHAPTER IV

Bibliography
Bolt, B.A, *Earthquakes,* W.H. Freeman, New York, 1988.

Bolt, B.A., Horn, W.L., Macdonald, G.A. and Scott, R.F., *Geological Hazards,* Springer-Verlag, Berlin 1975.

Coburn, A. and Spence, R., *Earthquake Protection,* John Wiley, Chichester, 1992.

Dowrick, D.J., *Earthquake Resistant Design for Engineers and Architects,* John Wiley, Chichester, 1987.

Wyllie, Bob, "Volunteers in emergencies in the UK", *Abstracts of the First International Congress on Local Authorities Confronting Disasters and Emergencies,* Union of Local Authorities in Israel, Tel-Aviv, 1994.

Ben Hador, Avi, "Special care for tourists at the time of disaster", *Abstracts of the First International Congress on Local Authorities Confronting Disasters and Emergencies,* Union of Local Authorities in Israel, Tel-Aviv, 1994.

Ting-Kuei, Tsay and Fang-Bin, Lin, "Confronting potential disasters of Taipei county area in Taiwan", *Abstracts of the First International Congress on Local Authorities Confronting Disasters and Emergencies,* Union of Local Authorities in Israel, Tel-Aviv, 1994.

Heath, Robert. "The Newcastle earthquake (1989): a shock to the system", *Abstracts of the First International Congress on Local Authorities Confronting Disasters and Emergencies,* Union of Local Authorities in Israel, Tel-Aviv, Israel, 1994.

Moore, Avagene. "Trends in emergency management", *Abstracts of the First International Congress on Local Authorities Confronting Disasters and Emergencies,* Union of Local Authorities in Israel, Tel-Aviv, Israel, 1994.

MacFarlane, Gordon J., "Emergency site management", *Abstracts of the First International Congress on Local Authorities Confronting Disasters and Emergencies,* Union of Local Authorities in Israel, Tel-Aviv, 1994.

Bar-On, Raphael R. and Paz-Tal, Gershon, "Minimising and measuring the effects of disasters on tourism", *Abstracts of the First International*

Congress on Local Authorities Confronting Disasters and Emergencies, Union of Local Authorities in Israel, Tel-Aviv, 1994.

Sonmez, S.F., Backman, S.J. and Allen, L.A., *Managing Tourism Crises: A Guidebook,* Department of Parks, Recreation and Tourism Management, Clemson University, Clemson, SC, USA, 1994.

Hayes, Peter. "The Management of an organization in crisis", *Abstracts of the First International Congress on Local Authorities Confronting Disasters and Emergencies,* Union of Local Authorities in Israel, Tel-Aviv, Israel, 1994.

Kreizelman, David, "The emergency press center in Tel Aviv during the Persian Gulf War", *Abstracts of the First International Congress on Local Authorities Confronting Disasters and Emergencies,* Union of Local Authorities in Israel, Tel-Aviv, Israel, 1994.

Feinberg, David, "Quest for ways to rescue people from collapsed modern structures", *Abstracts of the First International Congress on Local Authorities Confronting Disasters and Emergencies,* Union of Local Authorities in Israel, Tel-Aviv, Israel, 1994.

Additional sources

Littlejohn, R.F., *Crisis Management: A Team Approach,* American Management Association, New York, 1983.

Bates, R.J., *Disaster Recovery Planning,* McGraw-Hill, New York, 1992.

Berge, D.T., *The First 24 Hours,* Basil Blackwell, Cambridge, MA, USA, 1992.

Smith, J., *The Publicity Kit,* John Wiley, New York, 1991.

US Federal Emergency Management Agency, *Are You Ready?,* Publication H-34, Washington, DC, September 1993.

US Federal Emergency Management Agency, *Guide for the Development of State and Local Emergency Operations Plans,* Publication CPG 1-8, Washington, DC, September 1990.

US Federal Emergency Management Agency, *Home Study Course on The Emergency Program Manager,* Publication IS-1, Washington, DC, September 1993.

US Federal Emergency Management Agency, *Emergency Management Guide for Business & Industry,* Publication FEMA 141, Washington, DC, October 1993.

CHAPTERS V AND VI

Bibliography

Armstrong, B., Williams, K., *The Avalanche Book,* Golden, 1986.

Association suisse pour la défense contre les avalanches (ASDA), *Avalanche Protection in Switzerland,* General Technical report RM-9, CO, 1975.

Fraser, C., *The Avalanche Enigma,* Rand McNally, New York, 1966.

Frutiger, H., "History and actual state of legislation of avalanche zoning in Switzerland", *Journal of Glaciology,* Vol. 26, No. 94, 1980, P. 313-324.

US National Research Council, *Snow Avalanche Hazards and Mitigation in the United States,* National Academy Press, Washington, DC, 1990.

Perla, R., Martinelli, Jr, *Avalanche Handbook,* Agriculture Handbook 489, US Department of Agriculture Forest Service, 1976.

References

Wyllie, Bob. "Volunteers in emergencies in the UK", *Abstracts of the First International Congress on Local Authorities Confronting Disasters and Emergencies,* Union of Local Authorities in Israel, Tel-Aviv, Israel, 1994.

Ben Hador, Avi. "Special care for tourists at the time of disaster", *Abstracts of the First International Congress on Local Authorities Confronting Disasters and Emergencies,* Union of Local Authorities in Israel, Tel-Aviv, Israel, 1994.

Morris, Charles L. "Cyclone drill and staff action ", Le Touessrok Hotel, Trou d'Eau Douce, Mauritius. Personal Communication, June, 17, 1994.

Gerasimenko, Alexander M. "Theses of the report of the Chairman of Minsk City Council of Deputies", *Abstracts of the First International Congress on Local Authorities Confronting Disasters and Emergencies,* Union of Local Authorities in Israel, Tel-Aviv, Israel, 1994.

Ting-Kuei, Tsay and Fang-Bin, Lin. "Confronting potential disasters of Taipei county area in Taiwan", *Abstracts of the First International Congress on Local Authorities Confronting Disasters and Emergencies,* Union of Local Authorities in Israel, Tel-Aviv, Israel, 1994.

Heath, Robert. "The Newcastle earthquake (1989): a shock to the system", *Abstracts of the First International Congress on Local Authorities Confronting Disasters and Emergencies,* Union of Local Authorities in Israel, Tel-Aviv, Israel, 1994.

Moore, Avagene. "Trends in emergency management", *Abstracts of the First International Congress on Local Authorities Confronting Disasters and Emergencies,* Union of Local Authorities in Israel, Tel-Aviv, Israel, 1994.

MacFarlane, Gordon J. "Emergency site management", *Abstracts of the First International Congress on Local Authorities Confronting Disasters and Emergencies,* Union of Local Authorities in Israel, Tel-Aviv, Israel, 1994.

Norris, D.R. "The North Wales floods - 1990", *Abstracts of the First International Congress on Local Authorities Confronting Disasters and Emergencies,* Union of Local Authorities in Israel, Tel-Aviv, Israel, 1994.

Yuanpeng, Song. "Shanghai chemical emergency accident preparedness and rescue programme", *Abstracts of the First International Congress on Local Authorities Confronting Disasters and Emergencies,* Union of Local Authorities in Israel, Tel-Aviv, Israel, 1994.

Bar-On, Raphael R. and Paz-Tal, Gershon. "Minimising and measuring the effects of disasters on tourism", *Abstracts of the First International Congress on Local Authorities Confronting Disasters and Emergencies,* Union of Local Authorities in Israel, Tel-Aviv, Israel, 1994.

Sonmez, S.F., Backman, S.J. and Allen, L.A., *Managing Tourism Crises: A Guidebook,* Department of Parks, Recreation and Tourism Management, Clemson University, Clemson, SC, USA, 1994.

Hayes, Peter. "The Management of an organization in crisis", *Abstracts of the First International Congress on Local Authorities Confronting Disasters and Emergencies,* Union of Local Authorities in Israel, Tel-Aviv, Israel, 1994.

Kreizelman, David, "The emergency press center in Tel Aviv during the Persian Gulf War", *Abstracts of the First International Congress on Local*

Authorities Confronting Disasters and Emergencies, Union of Local Authorities in Israel, Tel-Aviv, Israel, 1994.

Feinberg, David, "Quest for ways to rescue people from collapsed modern structures", *Abstracts of the First International Congress on Local Authorities Confronting Disasters and Emergencies,* Union of Local Authorities in Israel, Tel-Aviv, Israel, 1994.